THE REAL READER'S QUARTERLY

# Slightly Foxed

## 'Tigers at the Double Lion'

NO.70 SUMMER 2021

*Editors* Gail Pirkis & Hazel Wood
*Marketing and publicity* Stephanie Allen & Jennie Harrison Bunning
*Bookshops* Anna Kirk
*Subscriptions* Hattie Summers & Jess Dalby

*Cover illustration:* Nicholas Hely Hutchinson, *From Mupe Bay to St Aldhelm's Head* (detail), oil on canvas, 32 x 60 in., reproduced courtesy of the artist and the Jerram Gallery, Sherborne, Dorset (www.jerramgallery.com)

Born in 1955, Nicholas Hely Hutchinson studied at St Martin's School of Art. Since his first exhibition in 1984 he has exhibited consistently in London, Dublin and Hong Kong, and his work is now in many private and corporate collections. 'I wake up most mornings thinking about painting. Usually it is something that I have seen the day before . . . A long straight sunlit road, lined with telegraph poles . . . A sparrow hawk flips over the hedge . . . These are possible elements for a picture. The seasons and the constantly changing moods of the countryside are my inspiration. A bird in a cold winter sky . . . This is what makes me want to paint . . . Moments of heart-breaking beauty, moments that take your breath away.'

*Back cover fox by Reynolds Stone*
*Design by Octavius Murray, layout by Andrew Evans,*
*colophon and tailpiece by David Eccles*

Published by Slightly Foxed Limited
53 Hoxton Square
London N1 6PB

tel 020 7033 0258
email office@foxedquarterly.com
www.foxedquarterly.com

*Slightly Foxed* is published quarterly in early March, June, September and December

Annual subscription rates (4 issues)
UK and Ireland £48; Overseas £56

Single copies of this issue can be bought for £12.50 (UK) or £14.50 (Overseas)

All back issues in printed form are also available

ISBN 978-1-910898-57-4
ISSN 1742-5794

*Printed and bound by Smith Settle, Yeadon, West Yorkshire*

# Contents

## Contents

John Watson

### The Slightly Foxed Podcast

A new episode of our podcast is available on the 15th of every month. To listen, visit www.foxedquarterly.com/pod or search for Slightly Foxed on Audioboom, iTunes or your podcast app.

### Subscriber Benefits

Slightly Foxed can obtain any books reviewed in this issue, whether new or second-hand. To enquire about a book, to access the digital edition of *Slightly Foxed* or to view a list of membership benefits, visit www.foxedquarterly.com/members or contact the office: 020 7033 0258/office@foxedquarterly.com.

# *From the Editors*

Looking back over the past strange and difficult months, it's cheering to see some of the good things that have come out of the 'new normal'. One is Bookshop.org, a website launched last autumn to enable independent bookshops to continue trading online through the pandemic, which generated £1 million profit for indie bookshops in its first four months. It has enabled many a struggling bookshop to avoid furloughing staff and help pay its running costs and we hope it will gather strength in the online fight to challenge the behemoth that is Amazon. Definitely worth checking out.

As to *Slightly Foxed*, we can only say yet again that the pandemic has shown us just how truly loyal *SF* readers are. We've been touched by the many ways in which you have shown your support, from thoughtful and encouraging messages to extra sales, and the podcasts have brought you and *SF* together in an especially meaningful way. Though we're still scattered when we record them, Philippa in Cambridge, Gail in Devon, Hazel and Anna in London, Steph in West Sussex and Jennie in her cottage on the Norfolk border, we're looking forward to getting together in the office again, and we feel optimistic about the future.

Having spent so much time looking at our own four walls, many of us are probably dreaming of a getaway somewhere this summer. But whether you're at home or away, this magic-carpet issue of *SF* will transport you much further, to distant places and other times, in the company of some fascinating writers. Among them, V. S. Naipaul takes us to Trinidad, Rose Macaulay to the shores of the Black Sea, Robert Graves to Rome in the days of the Emperor Claudius, and

Anthony Burgess to the seedy backstreets of Kuala Lumpur in the dying days of British colonial rule.

This season's new Slightly Foxed Edition is a memoir of a very unusual kind. It might even be described as a travel book, for in it the historian Richard Cobb, known for both his brilliant books on French history and his unconventional lifestyle, recreates in entrancing detail the Tunbridge Wells of his childhood in the 1920s and '30s, leading us through the town and into the lives of its inhabitants, from his mother's tweed-and-Jaeger clad bridge-playing friends to Baroness Olga, the town's only victim of the Russian Revolution. This quiet backwater, Cobb writes, was 'a society in which a rather frightened child could feel at home', and it's a great antidote to troubled times we think.

We're also reissuing another of our best-loved SFEs in a Plain Foxed Edition, *Look Back with Love* by the novelist Dodie Smith, best known as the author of *I Capture the Castle* and *The One Hundred and One Dalmatians*. Dodie grew up in Manchester's Victorian suburbs at the turn of the last century in the jolliest possible extended family. The Furbers adored seaside trips, motor-car outings, fairgrounds, circuses, jokes, charades and musical soirées, all of which had their influence on Dodie. Her memoir gives a marvellous picture of life in a large Edwardian family, and of the little girl who said, 'I'm an oddity really. But I do my very very best to write well.'

Perhaps the same might be said of dear *Slightly Foxed*. We look forward to the rest of a year that's full of plans and to seeing some of you in person again, we hope, at Readers' Day in November.

GAIL PIRKIS & HAZEL WOOD

# Tigers at the Double Lion

TIM MACKINTOSH-SMITH

While staying recently in Chiswick, I went on a literary pilgrimage to Glebe Street, where Anthony Burgess and his wife Lynn lived in the 1960s. I wasn't sure what I would do when I got to No. 24. Genuflect at the garden gate?

Halfway down the street, a triangulation took place. The postman came out of a front gate, a woman arrived from the opposite direction and stopped him, and I stepped aside to circumvent them. As I did so, I heard the woman say, 'Have you got anything for No. 24?'

Coincidence? It seemed more like a prearranged meeting. 'Oh!' I said. 'You live in Burgess's house!'

She too was a fan, and in the flush of the moment she invited me in for tea.

We should have had Burgessian triple gins and water, then gone on a pub crawl, got into fights, lost teeth. But I settled for gin and water without the gin, quicker to down than tea. I'd had the sudden realization that she might have decided I was a potential maniac.

'I don't normally invite strange men off the street like this,' she said. She obviously did think I was a maniac; I had better go. Before I did, I tried to take in my surroundings. The house had had makeovers but would have been easily recognizable to Burgess. It was very quiet. In the silence, I listened for Lynn, softly coughing her liver and her life away in the bedroom upstairs. Burgess had heard his wife's cough after

Anthony Burgess's Malayan trilogy, comprising *Time for a Tiger* (1956), *The Enemy in the Blanket* (1958) and *Beds in the East* (1959), is available in a single-volume paperback from Vintage (608pp · £12.99 · ISBN 9780749395926).

her death; Haji the border collie had pricked up his ears, too.

There was nothing. Only that negation of noise which is not silence but the sound of the flow of time.

\*

Here in Kuala Lumpur there is noise – the hum and buzz of an Asian city, thunder rumbling round a tropical forest of cranes and towers. Time has flowed fast.

Looking out of our Barbican-Brutalist condo, I wonder what Burgess would recognize if he made a ghostly visit to the land where he set his first three published novels, the books that made his name – literally: Anthony Burgess, in place of John Anthony Burgess Wilson. We are in his old KL carousing-ground, seedy Chow Kit. But KL is no longer 'Kouala L'impure', as Burgess claimed Cocteau dubbed it; there is nary a red light to be seen (or is it age that dims the sight?). There are, however, odd survivals: one is the Coliseum, down the road, where you can still get a decent colonial-era tiffin: 'a portion of fried fish, a steak with onions and chipped potatoes, a dish of chopped pineapple and tinned cream', washed down with Tiger beers. I would wager that Burgess peed a few pints into the Coliseum's Duchampesque urinals. (They are kept filled with ice cubes . . . Why? I asked the barman. 'To cool your balls, sir.' Burgess, chronically randy despite or because of Lynn, would have benefited.)

Otherwise, Burgess's Malayan trilogy seems to be set in a different world – in the low-rise ruins of the British Empire, suburban Piranesi with the 'snaky, leechy jungle' and its Communist terrorist denizens lurking on all sides, and National Service Tommies being vomited from bar to brothel. That other world is hyper-real. When Burgess pre-warns the reader (and the litigious) about the first of the trilogy, *Time for a Tiger* (1956), that 'The Malay state of Lanchap and its towns and inhabitants do not really exist', it is rather like Magritte declaring '*Ceci n'est pas une pipe.*' It is all of the utmost verisimilitude, with events copied and pasted direct from his and Lynn's six Malayan years in the 1950s. Admittedly the names are changed. Lanchap ('Masturbate') is Perak; Kenching ('Urine') of *The Enemy in the Blanket* (1958), the second volume, is Kota Bharu. In the third, *Beds in the East* (1959), the setting is unnamed, but events and characters are drawn no less from the life.

Burgess's Malaya, then, is impeccably authentic, despite the smutty schoolboy renamings. In contrast to Maugham, the outsider, and even Conrad, whose viewpoint was seaborne, he was there almost long enough to count as an old hand; certainly long enough to raise two fingers to colonial mores. The setting ought to be visitable. Yet whereas Glebe Street has had mere makeovers, Malaya seems to have undergone the total *Grand Designs* metamorphosis. The Malayan trilogy is a period piece.

But it is much more. It was written on a cusp in time, between the death of empire and the birth of nations, and, as Paul Bowles saw in Morocco and Lawrence Durrell in Cyprus, the demise of the 500-year European imperial project was a good point to write from. Things were falling apart and re-forming; change is the motor of literature as much as the subject of history. It was a time of bathos rather than pathos. One of Burgess's main characters sees the end of empire as *Götterdämmerung*; in truth, it was less Wagner than Gilbert & Sullivan. The Malayan trilogy may be fiction, then, but it is also eyewitness history. It ponders, too, on what is to come: the triptych ends with Malaya's independence, and with a glimpse of its future – one in which there is hope of inter-racial harmony in this 'exquisite, impossible country', but in which the new order would be 'based on racial mystique'. That is prescient.

The three novels also prognosticate Burgess's own future. His Malayan teddy boys – 'Punch him in the *bodek*,' they yell (those parts one cools at the Coliseum) – are elder brothers to the Nadsat-speaking droogs of *A Clockwork Orange*. Learning Malay, Burgess said, 'changed the whole shape of my mind'. His ears were opened to the strange music of words, not least words in his own native tongue:

'the brontoid dawn'; 'plenilunar buttocks'; an 'apneumatic bosom'. All this is classic Burgess.

Burgess himself realized that he 'came here as a teacher, but left as a writer' – a fully formed writer, ringmaster of settings and atmospheres, emotions and motivations, words, plot (which is another term for coincidences) and, best of all, characters. The *Observer* critic wrote of his 'splendidly mad' cast. We tend to think of imperial Brits as Newboltian rugger-buggers. Many of them were; many of them were, or went, clinically bonkers. Burgess's main character, Victor Crabbe, is quietly mad but not at all splendid: he teaches and adulterizes his way through the trilogy, central to the plot but crabwise to the action. Burgess denied that Crabbe was himself; he is, rather, an avatar, a self-generated plaything of a reckless imagination. The rest are gleefully splendid, and include Ibrahim, Crabbe's cross-dressing Malay houseboy, Fatimah Bibi, for whom kissing is 'the blackest sensual depravity', and Rosemary Michael, a pre-#MeToo peach serially wooed by perfidious Albionites, and serially jilted because of her Tamil hue; Burgess called the real-life Rosemary 'a true victim of imperialism'.

Most memorable of all is Nabby Adams, a shambolic giant of a policeman in the Transport Pool with a dog that answers to the name of 'Cough' (in strict orthography, ''Ck Off': her previous owner, Nabby explains apologetically, 'was always telling her to get from under his feet'). Ruinously fond of beer, Nabby is both holy innocent and tortured hero, 'Prometheus with the eagles of debt and drink pecking at his liver'. Strangely, he – a Northamptonshire sexton's son – is eloquent in Urdu, thanks to an unexplained past. Far from being some monster of Burgess's creation, he was closely based on a certain Donald D. 'Lofty' Dunkeley. We forget that empire threw up such marvellous mutations.

With many others, they make up a Hieronymus Bosch crowd of grotesques. It is all mad indeed – Kipling on speed, Willie Maugham on laughing gas. It could also have been anarchic, but Burgess was a deft orchestrator of themes and forms; it helped that he had been a composer before he was a writer. The theme of the trilogy's first movement is music's great accompanist, booze. Burgess claimed he applied for the Malaya job when drunk, then forgot about it until summoned to the interview. In Malaya he went on as he began. *Time for a Tiger* is the beeriest book imaginable, with its constant refrain of 'Tiger, Anchor, Carlsberg'. The title itself was a slogan on advertising clocks supplied to *kedais*, Chinese shops-cum-bars. Nabby is 'six feet eight inches of thirst'; beer is 'his houri, his paramour', offering 'euphoria far beyond the release of detumescence'. I once unwisely read the book in a period when I was deprived of booze, and it made me physically ache for beer. Even thinking of the title still produces a Pavlovian response, an irresistible craving to put a Tiger in my tankard.

From drink to food. *The Enemy in the Blanket* is filled with maniacal menus and fatal feasts, like the 'Edwardian luncheons' of Crabbe's cook, Ah Wing: 'ox-tail soup, grilled sole, Scotch eggs, beef and four vegetables, caramel cream, Camembert'. And not only does Ah Wing's cooking form part of the plot, it also explains history, for, in its very indigestibility, 'a tradition had been preserved in order to humiliate. Perhaps it really was time the British limped out of Malaya.' *A Clockwork Orange* would be dystopic; this is dyspeptic.

In *Beds in the East*, it is Burgess's great formative passion – music

– that pervades the story. A young Chinese prodigy has written a *Malayan Symphony*. Will the fusion of classical Western symphonic form and traditional Eastern content ever be played? Or will Malaya sell out to the jukebox, the Platters and a global-American future? Music resounds through the book, as it would in many of Burgess's later works. Orgasm is marked *ffff*; grief is notated with an allusion to Honegger; booze and music mix in 'the great Brahmsian movement of the sixth glass'. And, towards the close of the book, when Crabbe penetrates the *hulu*, the upriver heart of Malayan darkness, music, empire, plot, life all fall apart as disordered 78 rpm discs on a radiogram play fragments of Elgar, Parry and Dame Clara Butt. It is the aleatoric end of the imperial backing-track, Conrad in the age of *Naked Lunch*.

So, no: this is no mere period piece. Nor is it mere comic opera. It is a record of and reflection on the most traumatic age in Britain's recent history, an age whose repercussions we still live with today.

*

In real life it was Burgess himself, not the Chinese boy, who composed a *Sinfoni Melayu* (never to be performed). Returning in 1980, he bemoaned the fact that Malaysia had Barbara Cartland novels in the bookshops and *Dallas* on TV, but still no symphony orchestra. The jukebox had triumphed.

Forty years on, though, there *is* a symphony orchestra, the Malaysian Philharmonic. Time has fleshed out Burgess's ghosts of Malaya's future, his dream of a multicultural nation. But I still wanted to look for ghosts of Malaya's past, and particularly for Burgess's own spirit. Kuala Lumpur has been exorcized by the sheer velocity of its escape from the twentieth century, but I felt I would find something in the capital of Burgess's Lanchap, Kuala Hantu (*hantu* is 'ghost'). Kuala Kangsar, the real-life Kuala Hantu, is a backwater, and in the slow provincial flow of time, ghosts might have clung on. I went on another pilgrimage.

The physical backdrop was little changed. There was the Malay

College, the 'Eton of the East', where Burgess taught – inspiration for Crabbe's Mansor College. There was the Idris Club, Crabbe's Iblis ('Devil') Club, where one drank when not slumming it. And there, on a rise above the *kuala*, or confluence, was the King's Pavilion, where Burgess and Crabbe had lived. I looked up at the top-floor veranda where Nabby would snore the night away on a Bombay fornicator, knocked out by Crabbe's booze. Somewhere within was a literally haunted bathroom, where unspeakable things had happened during the Japanese occupation. Was it still haunted? It was now a girls' school, so as good as impenetrable.

The Idris Club, closed for the day, was impenetrable too, but I eventually found a *kedai*, the Double Lion. The Tigers were slightly warm; Nabby would have approved – iced beer to him was 'effeminate . . . and American'. In the first eucharistic euphoria of alcohol, and for the first time since I had arrived, Burgess suddenly seemed a real presence. But as the Tigers tightened their hold, I realized it was wishful thinking. The only spectre here was me, pale visitant from a distant isle. The only sort of time that flowed was Tiger time – and it all ended in the Universal Urinal, that bourn from which no pilsener returns. The ghosts had gone. Only books, solidified memory, remained.

*

Back in KL, writing this, I have just looked at the Malayan section of Burgess's autobiography. In it I find that Burgess and Lofty used to drink 'warm Tiger beer *in the Double Lion kedai . . .*'

Coincidence?

Maybe there are no coincidences, only patterns we can't make out because we're lost in the geometry.

TIM MACKINTOSH-SMITH's most recent book, *Arabs: A 3,000-Year History of Peoples, Tribes and Empires*, was published by Yale in 2019. As a historian, he sees the absence of a blue plaque on Burgess's only London house as a grave omission and trusts the injustice will be remedied forthwith. The lady at No. 24 (who kindly assures TM-S that she didn't think he was a maniac) and the other good literary folk of Chiswick are doing their best.

# 'Delighted' of Tunbridge Wells

DAVID GILMOUR

Richard Cobb's first book in English was *A Second Identity* (1969), a title he chose to show how a middle-class Englishman became not just a historian of France but a historian who effectively became French, a man who had learned to say and even *feel* different things on opposite sides of the Channel. He had spent many years in Paris, living in *arrondissements* on both banks of the Seine, carrying out a prodigious amount of research in the Archives Nationales, and writing almost always in French. He was chuffed when Frenchmen mistook his nationality. '*Vous êtes Belge?*' they might ask, or better still, '*Vous êtes du Nord?*' for he loved to be thought a native of the textile towns of Lille or Roubaix.

Cobb was not a normal student working towards a doctorate; until the age of 38 he made no effort to acquire an academic post or indeed any other job. His life was anarchical (though not in any political sense) and unstructured. Classless in his new identity, he mixed easily with Parisians and provincials, Communists and Catholics, with prostitutes in the rue St Denis and petty criminals in Les Halles, with legionnaires or railway workers in a *tabac* in Rouen or Lyon. Yet this rather chaotic and bohemian life, fuelled by much carousing and plenty of red wine, did not prevent him from writing four long and impressive volumes on the French Revolution in French.

I knew Richard Cobb in the early 1970s, first as my tutor at Oxford and then as a friend until his death in 1996. By the early years of this period he had reverted to his first identity and become an Englishman who was a professor who now wrote his books (also excellent, also on the Revolution) in English. Yet even as he acquired fame he remained anarchical, disruptive – and very funny. He received the Légion d'honneur; he won the Wolfson Prize; he was chairman of the judges of the Booker Prize; and at a dinner at Buckingham Palace he drank too much and had to be escorted out down a back staircase.

I thought I knew both identities, the second during occasional meetings in Paris where I lived for a while and where, after a convivial dinner, I would walk him to his lodgings off the rue St Antoine only to find that he could not remember where he was staying on that particular evening; it was after quite a lot of random bell-pushing that we would find the right place.

Yet during those years Cobb was slowly revealing yet another identity, or perhaps it was more a mutation of the first: the sensitive English boy from the provincial south-east, from Kent and Essex, a child with an insatiable desire to explore the unromantic townscapes of those counties. (It was of course wonderfully inappropriate that he should have been born, in 1917, in Frinton, a town which did not possess a single pub in the whole of the twentieth century.) As someone who had loved to share a bottle of *vin rouge* with him in a café on the boulevards, I was rather shocked when he wrote to me about his 'beloved Manningtree' and confessed that he had never felt 'more English, more Protestant or more middle class'.

For some time he had been inserting little bits of autobiography into the prefaces of his most memorable books on French history. In *Reactions to the French Revolution* he introduced his Uncle Primus, a person with no connection to France or indeed anywhere really except Colchester where, in the house of his parents, he led a life of stupefying routine, winding the clock, laying the table, tapping the barometer and reading the *Essex Standard*; he did no conventional work, except making some rugs, and after the death of his parents he moved to a boarding-house in Clacton-on-Sea where he went mad.

Impatient readers might wonder what on earth Uncle Primus had to do with characters in the book such as a water-carrier from Aveyron or a market porter from Brittany. Not much, of course, except that Cobb liked to write about 'ordinary', unremarkable people. Essential to his approach to writing history was his stress on the importance and the independence of individuals, of their idiosyncrasies, their sufferings, the banality of their existences – and his sympathy for people trying as far as possible to lead normal lives in times of war and revolution.

In 1980 Cobb gave Uncle Primus (and other relations) a more extended outing in 'The House on the Hythe', a chapter in *Places*, a book edited by Ronald Blythe, the author of *Akenfield*. Its success persuaded him to make further excursions into autobiography, whole books now, and still concentrating very much on south-east England. All his life he liked flat country: Essex and Suffolk, Flanders and the Pas de Calais. He never liked hills ('they spoil the view'), and he particularly disliked Scotland, where I used to live; on the map, he said, it looked as if it had been torn out of a piece of paper. For him the country's only advantage was that its climate and topography made it unsuitable for cricket, a game that he hated.

The first and best of these memoirs is *Still Life: Sketches from a Tunbridge Wells Childhood* (1983), a book I have read half a dozen times. I do not know a more evocative account of a childhood, of the place in which it was lived or of the many and very varied people one encounters during it. The book displays Cobb's great skills – as an observer, as a social historian, as a man with an extraordinary power of recall, and a writer with a unique style of prose and a remarkable sense of place.

Richard moved to Tunbridge Wells at the age of 4 with his mother and sister; his father, who was in the Sudan Civil Service, was only an intermittent presence until his retirement. The family moved house a good deal, from one rented place to another, but managed to retain its status among the many gradations of middle-class society in a very middle-class town. Mr Cobb did not care much about status – he was happiest in his allotment chatting with whoever was digging

The Pantiles, Tunbridge Wells, early 1920s

in the neighbouring potato patch – but Mrs Cobb did. She was a sensible, good-hearted and harmlessly snobbish woman, who played cards at the Ladies' Bridge Club with the widows of colonial officials and (as a doctor's daughter) relished the exclusion of dentists from the Nevill Tennis Club.

As a child observer who was curious, unpretentious and above all empathetic, Richard was the perfect person to portray Tunbridge Wells and its peculiar society. His ear for dialogue and social nuance is wonderfully displayed in a description of a party of ladies, 'hatted and gloved', returning by train from Charing Cross after a shopping jaunt to Harrods and Swan & Edgar. How well he captures the voices and accentuations – something was 'simply *frightful*', someone was a 'little *hussy*', someone else was 'a bit *brainy*' (in a negative and possibly even dangerous way) – and their appearances, the scarves, the blouses, the thick stockings, 'the washed-out, blue eyes . . . the clearly-marked deltas of mauve veins [and] extensive estuaries . . . that gave to their weather-beaten red faces a hint of intelligence and even kindness'.

Cobb was a spectator, a witness, not a mocker or a satirist. He devotes several pages to a family of distant cousins, the Limbury-Buses, a group of very idle people who managed to insulate themselves from the world, even in the middle of the Second World War. They hardly did anything except consume cucumber sandwiches and go for very short walks; they certainly did not listen to the wireless to find out how the war was going. Yet however boring they must have been, Cobb is not censorious. I think he rather admired their imperturbability.

Richard may have been eccentric, irreverent and anarchical but he was also someone who needed reassurance. He needed a place that would reassure him that life, however threatening it might be elsewhere, could carry on. For him his childhood town was that place, at least until his mother died. In September 1939 he was playing Bridge in his parents' drawing-room when he felt a sudden 'cold anguish' about the coming war. Thinking of his participation and possible death, he panicked, played a wrong card and lost the trick. Then he stared out of the French windows at the town with its hills and its monkey-puzzle trees, looked around the room at the familiar family objects, felt the tranquil and reassuring presence of his parents – and calmed down. Nothing too terrible, he managed to convince himself, could ever happen to him in Royal Tunbridge Wells.

A quarter of a century after Richard Cobb's death, DAVID GILMOUR still misses talking, eating and drinking with him. In 1998 he edited two volumes of Cobb's writings, *The French and Their Revolution* and *Paris and Elsewhere*.

Richard Cobb's *Still Life: Sketches from a Tunbridge Wells Childhood* (224pp) is now available in a limited and numbered cloth-bound edition of 2,000 copies (subscribers: UK & Eire £18, Overseas £20; non-subscribers: UK & Eire £19.50, Overseas £21.50). All prices include post and packing. Copies may be ordered by post (53 Hoxton Square, London N1 6PB), by phone (020 7033 0258) or via our website www.foxedquarterly.com.

# Food without Shame

OLIVIA POTTS

In my baking cupboard, at the very back of the top shelf, there is an open bag of wheatgerm. It has survived one house move and more than six years of ownership, and it is depleted by only one loaf's worth. Laurie Colwin is to blame.

I first read Colwin's *Home Cooking* (1988) right at the start of my journey into food and cooking, long before I'd jacked in my career to train as a pâtisserie chef. At the time, I'd never baked a loaf. In one of the essays in that book – 'Bread baking without agony' – Colwin describes her own first foray into baking, in which a friend guided her through an exhausting day of proving, kneading and shaping. She wrote, 'The result was a perfectly nice loaf of bread, but after spending an entire day in its service, I expected something a little more heroic.'

This candour marks much of Colwin's writing and, as someone new to the food world, I found it deeply refreshing. She wasn't romantic or pretentious about food, as other food writers were. She was honest and practical, and she didn't stand on culinary ceremony. She found another way to bake bread, one which allowed her to fit the bread around her life, rather than the other way round. This sounded more like my kind of cooking. So I

Laurie Colwin, *Home Cooking* (1988) · Fig Tree · Pb · 208pp · £12.99 · ISBN 9780241145715; *More Home Cooking* (1993) is out of print but we can obtain second-hand copies.

followed her recipe, even going so far as to track down the wheat-germ that she used, which I eventually found in a health-food shop (and never again encountered in a bread recipe) – and much to my surprise, I ended up with a delicious loaf of bread. Imbued with a newfound confidence, I quickly moved on to other recipes, hence the forgotten wheatgerm. But without Laurie Colwin, I would never have got started.

Laurie Colwin was an American writer who produced five novels, three collections of short stories and two volumes of essays and recipes, *Home Cooking* and *More Home Cooking* (1993). She wrote for the *New Yorker* and was a regular and much-loved contributor to *Gourmet* and *Mademoiselle* magazines, where her columns focused on the intersection of food and life. Her kitchen essays have a cultish following in the food world – *Home Cooking* was posthumously admitted to the illustrious James Beard Cookbook Hall of Fame – but her work is not nearly as widely known as it deserves to be.

Long before Nigella's *Kitchen* and Nigel Slater's *Kitchen Diaries* invited us into their homes, mixing personal narrative with domestic culinary instruction, there was Colwin. She was the original 'writer in the kitchen' (which happens to be the subtitle of *Home Cooking*), the proto-food memoirist – conversational, untrained and inexact, but with buckets of enthusiasm and practical nous.

If it sounds diminishing to describe her as a 'domestic' writer, then it shouldn't. This was the realm in which she revelled and which she championed. As she put it, 'It is not just the Great Works of mankind that make a culture. It is the daily things, like what people eat and how they serve it.' Food is life, and Colwin served hers up with jokes and trivia, delightful diversions and strange segues. She wrote about her husband and small child, and her 'Lilliputian' apartment which witnessed both her dinner parties and her hangovers. She illuminated what it was like to be a woman in her own kitchen in a serious way, but without ever taking herself too seriously.

She was also, to me at least, laugh-out-loud funny. Consider her reflections on a friend's neat shelf of preserves:

> There is nothing more daunting than to visit someone's country house and see a jelly cupboard actually filled with homemade jam and jelly, neatly labelled, row upon row. I once visited a classic supermom on an island in Maine: no running water, no electricity. One wood stove and an outhouse. Above her stove was rigged a massive jelly bag, which dripped into a kettle. She and her children had collected wild apples, and she was making a jelly out of them. *I am a worm,* I thought to myself.

Her essay titles themselves speak volumes: 'Desserts that quiver', 'Jam anxiety', 'Turkey angst', 'Alone in the kitchen with an eggplant'.

She was also extraordinarily perceptive about the ways in which people actually cook and eat. 'If you ask an experienced cook what dish is foolproof, scrambled eggs is often the answer. But the way toward perfect scrambled eggs is full of lumps.' Instead, Colwin offers a simple beef stew, which is truly a far easier thing for a kitchen novice to master. When she writes about the amateur cook going into the kitchen 'armed with a *chinois* and a copy of *Edwardian Glamour Cooking without Tears* in order to produce a lobster bisque', I feel as if she's watching me at 25 trying to host a dinner party.

Colwin has opinions, but she is disarmingly self-aware about them being just that. 'As everyone knows, there is only one way to fry chicken correctly. Unfortunately, most people think their method is best, but most people are wrong. Mine is the only right way, and on this subject I feel almost evangelical.' This is the kind of authority that compelled me to buy that bag of wheatgerm. She is both eminently practical and – for a control freak like me – maddeningly elliptical, instructing the reader to 'Make the polenta in the ordinary way' or 'Boil the potatoes – the amount depends on how many people you are feeding'. I suspect that few of her devotees read her for her recipes. It may have been her recipe that propelled me into bread-making, but now, with more experience under my belt, her laissez-faire instruction in that very recipe – 'You can preheat the oven or put it in a cold oven, it matters not a bit' – is enough to give me conniptions.

Perhaps my favourite thing about her is that she, like me, was greedy. It's always refreshing to read about a woman who loves food without shame. Here she is on roasting turkey for Thanksgiving: 'A nicer person would throw in the neck, but I am not a nice person, and I roast the neck, which I then eat all by myself in the kitchen without a trace of guilt, because I did all the work.'

Colwin's practicality is reinforced by the elegant economy of her prose, where a throwaway phrase often serves to paint a vast canvas. Writing about Thanksgiving, and the need to tailor how you serve your turkey to the number of guests, she sums up with one word something that took Proust 4,000 pages: 'Although turkey is delicious in itself, it is burdened with *context.*'

Colwin was an Anglophile through and through, particularly when it came to food writing. She adored Jane Grigson, Margaret Costa and Elizabeth David (as well as Edna Lewis and Marcella Hazan). One of her favourite novelists was Barbara Pym. Her love for old-fashioned English food is deeply endearing; her first encounter with double cream – something not really found in America – is one of my favourites. She cannot identify the immovable thick-enough-to-stand-a-spoon substance in the jug. 'This is *cream?*' she gasps. So enamoured with it is she that she persuades (or bullies) a friend to bring a pot of double cream in his hand luggage when he flies to America. He emerges from Customs 'carrying a dripping bag out in front of him as if it were a wet fish. His coat sleeves and his shoes were covered in double cream. Predictably, the lid had slipped and covered him in cream in transit; the customs officials spoke gently, as if to an insane person. "We have dairy products in the United States, too, Mr Davies."'

The peculiarities of English food also precipitated one of Colwin's finest passages, in which she takes a Sussex pond pudding as a slightly unusual hostess gift. For the uninitiated, Sussex pond pudding is a very old-fashioned British recipe in which a whole lemon and large quantities of butter and sugar are boiled inside a suet pastry case, the lemon infusing the sauce that forms inside the pastry. 'It never occurred to me that nobody might want to eat it . . . My hostess looked confused. "It looks like a baked hat . . ."' But poor feedback never seemed to bother Colwin. 'The others ate ice cream. I ate almost the entire pudding myself.'

Mrs Beeton's Sussex
pudding basin

In fact, Colwin is probably at her most engaging when describing her culinary disasters – a topic that most food writers avoid, bar one benign example to show that they are as fallible as the rest of us. By contrast, she reels them off with something approaching pride. 'When it finally emerged from the oven, this fish looked like Hieronymus Bosch's vision of hell, with little nasty-looking things spilling out into a pallid-looking puddle of undercooked fish juices.' Or consider her attempt at meat fondue:

> While we waited we ate up all the bread and butter. One of the Alices began to eat the béarnaise sauce with a spoon. The other Alice suggested we go out for dinner. Once in a while we would dip a steak cube into the oil to see what happened. At first we pulled out oil-covered steak. After a while, the steak turned faintly gray. Finally, I turned one of my burners on high and put the pot on the burner to get it started. Thereafter we watched with interest as our steak cubes sizzled madly and turned into little lumps of rubbery coal . . . Then we went to the local bar for hamburgers and French fries.

Laurie Colwin died in 1992 of an aneurysm. She was 48. When Ruth Reichl became editor-in-chief of *Gourmet* in 1999, she found in her office 400 letters of mourning sent in by readers. While I was trying to find out more about her, I came across an article in the *New York Times* from 2014 entitled 'A confidante in the kitchen'. Beneath the article were hundreds of comments from people all over the world who hadn't known her but felt as though they did. They talked about her kitchen essays much more than her novels. And they actively missed her.

This is how I feel, too. Laurie Colwin was an extraordinarily skilled memoirist – it's impossible to read her and not feel as if you know her. The way she wrote about food feels like a direct precursor to a whole movement of cookery writing by food writers who welcome us into their homes. That's what *Home Cooking* is really about: home. A warm, welcoming place, with bread in the oven and soup on the stove. As Colwin wrote, 'No one who cooks cooks alone. Even at her most solitary, a cook in the kitchen is surrounded by generations of cooks past, the advice and menus of cooks present, the wisdom of cookbook writers.' This is how I felt as I made that first faltering loaf of bread, and that feeling is still with me.

OLIVIA POTTS is an award-winning food writer and the *Spectator*'s cookery columnist. Her first book, *A Half Baked Idea*, is available now.

# *When in Rome . . .*

ROBIN BLAKE

The older boy's name was Squire. I was 14 and reading in the house study under the Honours Board, with its gilded list of those who had left school with Oxbridge scholarships. My paperback, brand-new from the school bookshop, was *The Twelve Caesars* by Suetonius, in its imperial purple Penguin Classics livery. I was a few pages into the life of Julius when Squire came up behind me and snatched the book out of my hands.

'This is a dirty book, Blake.'

'No it's not. It's Roman history.'

His nostrils twitched in disapproval.

'It's dirty Roman history, and it's confiscated.'

He put the book in his pocket.

How could bloody Squire confiscate a book that I'd bought, with my own money, *in the school bookshop?* Because he was a bloody House Monitor and knew he could do as he liked! The injustice stung, and it still does.

Actually I was well aware that Suetonius was a bit racy – in particular the chapters on Tiberius, Caligula and Nero – but regretfully I had not yet reached the salacious bits. Anyway, they were not the prime reason I'd bought the book. I'd just finished Robert Graves's Claudius novels and wanted to look at one of their principal sources, which Graves had himself translated for Penguin. And the reason I wanted to do that was because *I, Claudius* (1934) and *Claudius the*

Robert Graves's *I, Claudius* (1934) and *Claudius the God* (1934) are both available as Penguin paperbacks, as is his translation of Suetonius's *The Twelve Caesars*.

*God* (1934) had kept me profoundly gripped in every spare moment for a good half of that term.

For several years before this I'd been slightly addicted to the Roman Empire. I used to pore over historical atlases tracing its rise, decline and fall, rather like a young zoologist getting hooked on the life cycle of the hippopotamus. I had been to the Roman Museum at York (known to me as Eboracum) and had become an expert on the fighting tackle of a legionary. I could talk knowledgeably about *denarii*, *solidi* and *sestertii* and had recently devoured Leonard Cottrell's bestselling history of Hannibal's invasion of Italy, *Enemy of Rome*. So when the Claudius books appeared, as orange Penguins at 3/6d, I immediately shelled out the necessary *solidi*.

Robert Graves himself had never been particularly crazy about the Romans, but he was given a solid classical grounding at Charterhouse and, when he found himself in need of cash, it was to first-century Rome that he turned. It was the early 1930s, and he was living on Majorca with the formidable, dangerous American writer Laura Riding. *Goodbye to All That*, his memoir of the Great War, had been a bestseller but he was in need of another success to fund his and Riding's Spanish house-building, and to support his abandoned first wife Nancy and their children.

The two books take the form of the intimate memoirs of Claudius himself, telling of his unlikely ascent to the imperial throne, and his surprisingly successful thirteen-year reign. Previously he had been known around Rome as Claudius the Idiot, or Clau-Clau-Claudius the Stammerer, and regarded as being in general an axe short of the full *fasces*. After his death the younger Seneca wrote a satire on Claudius's death, *The Pumpkinification of Claudius*, in which the Emperor dies giving a noisy fart and saying, 'Oh, good heavens, I believe I've made a mess of myself.' 'Whether this is actually so I can't say,' writes Seneca, 'but all agree that he always made a mess of things.'

For a long time historians had no more respect for Claudius than Seneca had – Edward Gibbon called him 'the most stupid of all the emperors' – but by the twentieth century opinion had shifted. The influential *Encyclopaedia Britannica*, in its celebrated 1911 edition, says that Claudius was an able administrator and stabilizing hand who rescued the empire from the tyranny of Tiberius and the ravages of Caligula. He was also 'a liberal-minded man of kindly nature anxious for the welfare of his people'. I am sure Graves read that brief article: it looks like a draft outline of his Claudius novels.

There was a stock character in Plautus's Roman comedies known as the Cunning Slave, outwardly dim and servile but inwardly a great schemer and survivor. That is Graves's Claudius, but with added self-deprecating humour and charm. He suffered from a number of handicaps, including a deaf ear after measles, a partially withered leg from polio, the aforementioned stammer and what I suppose we would now call Autism Spectrum Disorder. The suggestion of ASD may derive from Suetonius, who writes that the Emperor was 'so careless in what he said, it was thought he never reflected on who he himself was, or amongst whom, or at what time, or in what place he was speaking'. The fact that Graves's character is both detail-oriented and prodigally indiscreet, with some highly individual added quirks, shows how far Graves took Suetonius's characterization as a model.

Claudius was born into the Claudian family and so carried the genes of both Julius Caesar and Mark Antony in his DNA. A running motif in the story is that his family is split into Good Claudians and Bad Claudians, of whom the Bad not only outnumber the Good but generally tread them underfoot, then banish, bully, persecute, plot against and poison them. That is what happens to the two Good Claudians whom the narrator most admires, his father Drusus Nero and his brother Germanicus. The most poisonous Bad Claudian – in every sense – is Livia, wife and power behind the throne of the first emperor Augustus. Livia is a villain in the mould of Lady Macbeth and Lucrezia Borgia – manipulative in getting her way while making the Emperor think *he* made the decision. An important factor is that the God-Emperor, though he adores Livia, literally wilts as soon as he gets into bed with her. She exploits this by acting as procuress, providing him with a supply of nubile female flesh to fill the void.

Livia levers Tiberius, her son by a previous husband, into the succession. He has been an effective soldier but proves, in power, to be another Bad Claudian, his twenty-three-year reign descending into tyranny and gross dissipation. Written in the early 1930s, Graves's account of the political terror instigated by Livia and Tiberius looks like an uncanny copybook for the purges of Stalin and Beria that began just a few years later in the Soviet Union. First come the informers and the torture, then the accusations of treachery based on jokes or incidental remarks about the Emperor, followed by show trials in front of the Senate, in which the accused are forced to admit their guilt. Finally there are the banishings, the forced suicides and the brutal executions.

In one case that Claudius recounts in detail an unassuming senator is overheard by a snitch declining to explain to his wife some graffiti in which reference is made to a homicidal drunkard. Hauled before Tiberius, the poor fellow is forced to admit the thought-crime of believing the graffiti is about the Emperor, whereupon his cowed fellow senators sentence him to be hurled from the Tarpeian cliff, 'a punishment reserved for the worst traitors'. Under the Tiberian regime the slightest slip of the tongue can mean death and, as one character puts it, 'complacent anticipation of the monarch's wishes' is the only worthwhile political skill left.

In the latter part of his reign Tiberius retires to Capri, with the fixed idea of reviving his flagging sexual powers. The Caprian goings-on are detailed by Suetonius with greater specificity than by Graves's Claudius, which is exactly why I found my book being expropriated by the House Monitor at school. Not that there is anything erotic about the account in either book. *I, Claudius* makes it clear these are dour, joyless, sadistic sex-ercises, involving adults and children, of both genders and neither, whether willing or (more often) forced.

Tiberius's successor Caligula comes to power in his twenties, and reigns for just three years of insane extravagance and excess, in which his favourite horse is appointed Consul (akin to a Prime Minister) and he himself undergoes what he tells Claudius is a 'metamorphosis' into a living god. Temples, prayers and ceremonies are instigated, with observance being enforced on pain of very painful death. Caligula is the archetypal fun-loving psychopath: Brett Easton Ellis's Patrick Bateman in a toga and with unlimited powers.

Through all this Claudius crouches as best he can below the parapet but he is often dragged up into the firing line. Caligula likes to have Uncle Clau-Clau-Claudius around as a butt for his distinctly Bullingdon Club-like jokes. But Caligulan joking always has its sinister side and, more than once, Claudius seems to be heading for the Tarpeian cliff himself.

Caligula's ghastly antics are very entertaining, but the reader is delighted when he is assassinated and Claudius to his amazement is put on the throne. He is supposed to be a stop-gap – a pliable Emperor who will ease the way back to republican rule. Indeed his own inclinations are that way, but he quickly realizes the empire needs deep-reaching reforms and an economic revival before any change is possible. He determines to take on the job.

*Claudius the God*, which picks up the story at this point, is subtitled *. . . and His Wife Messalina*, but Messalina herself never quite comes to life in the way that Livia has done. Possibly Graves was inhibited by her historical notoriety as the paradigm of a rapacious *femme fatale*. We are aware of her sexual and political activities early on (no point in concealing what the reader already knows) and Claudius portrays himself as a hapless besotted January to her scheming and wildly promiscuous May, he being 50 and she only 15 when they marry at Caligula's mischievous bidding. The only reason Claudius offers for his failure to see through Messalina is her beauty and his blind, devouring love.

The first hundred pages of *Claudius the God* consist of what amounts to a subplot involving the adventures of Claudius's childhood friend, the Jewish prince Herod Agrippa, who is the grandson of the biblical Herod the Great. Herod Agrippa is a Byronic figure for Claudius, an adventurer but with his ear to the ground and a good head on his shoulders. He provides Claudius with useful counsel but, after burning bright as a rocket, comes like so many characters in the Claudius novels – actually almost *all* the characters – to a sorry end.

The big set-piece of the book is the invasion of Britain in which, with the help of war-elephants, the British king Caractacus is defeated in a battle witnessed by the Emperor and described by Graves the old soldier with great brio. At the end, says Claudius, 'we reached Colchester and . . . I travelled on elephant-back like an Indian Prince'. The final struggle with Messalina is then played out. She loses, but by now Claudius's spirit is broken and during the period when he is notionally writing his memoirs he has largely withdrawn from government. The narrative can't encompass Claudius's own death, so Graves rounds off the book with some Roman accounts of it, including Seneca's satire and an extract from Suetonius.

So ends what might be classified as one of the best potboilers ever written in English. It has always been revered. Three years after its publication Claudius almost won Graves the Nobel Prize ('What a waste of false modesty,' commented Riding) and, while Alexander Korda's film starring Charles Laughton and Merle Oberon was never completed, the BBC's 1970s serialization in which Derek Jacobi played Claudius was an international success. The books themselves have never been out of print.

And, by the way, in the meantime, I did never get my *Twelve Caesars* back.

ROBIN BLAKE is the author of seven mystery novels about the eighteenth-century coroner Titus Cragg and his forensic friend Dr Luke Fidelis.

# The Shining City

AMANDA THEUNISSEN

Picture the scene: a heavyweight London literary event in the 1930s. Two well-known women novelists, chatting. 'My novels won't live, Ivy,' says Rose Macaulay to Ivy Compton-Burnett. 'Yours may.'

How wrong she was on both counts. Ivy Compton-Burnett's novels, much admired in their time, have disappeared even from the shelves of charity shops. She found her style early and stuck to it and when she went out of fashion, there she stayed. Dame Rose Macaulay (as she became) has been overshadowed by her more famous contemporaries, appearing now on the edges of other people's stories. But as a writer and in her life she was an adventurous risk-taker, forever trying something different.

She wrote her first novel in 1906, followed by twenty-two more, and finally in 1956 her masterpiece, *The Towers of Trebizond*. Though early critics found it puzzling (surely Rose Macaulay wrote comic novels, what to make of this?) it has survived triumphantly. I think it's a great book, wise, light-hearted, funny – and very sad. I've read it many times and always find something different to absorb me.

It's a book that defies categorization. Semi-autobiographical (Macaulay referred to it as 'my own story'), it has a first-person narrator, Laurie. An ill-assorted group – a high Anglican priest, Laurie's Aunt Dot with her camel, and a Turkish woman academic – are on a road trip through Turkey to the Russian border, their aim to convert Turkish Muslim women to Christianity. Aunt Dot and Father

Rose Macaulay, *The Towers of Trebizond* (1956)
Flamingo · Pb · 288pp · £10.99 · ISBN 9780006544210

Chantry Pigg disappear into Russia, while Laurie returns to Trebizond to wait for her aunt, has some drug-induced visions of its imperial past (five centuries earlier it had been the last unconquered fragment of the Byzantine Empire) and then rides the camel to Israel where she meets her married lover, Vere. There's also a sub-plot about literary plagiarism and the ongoing saga of Aunt Dot's Russian escapade.

That's a brief summary of two-thirds of the book – impossible to do justice to the jokes, sharp observations and general gaiety. Part of its distinctive flavour comes from the many digressions. I am a second-hand scholar but Macaulay was a real one. I much admire the way she can start a section with, say, the pleasure of fishing for Black Sea turbot and end, via early Church history and landscapes, with a query about the kind of honey that drove Xenophon's 10,000 mad. She never loses her way. Her friends said this was how she chatted, skipping with light erudition from one interesting, tenuously connected subject to the next.

In the early stages *The Towers of Trebizond* could be mistaken for a travel book, which it definitely isn't, unless you consider riding a slightly mad white camel through Turkey, Syria and Jordan a realistic proposition. It becomes clear that although the book pulls in all the things Macaulay found most interesting – travel, history and legends; magic, ruins, the BBC, folk music, fishing, women's emancipation, wild swimming, food, literary scandals and gossip – the main thrust is the conflict between earthly love and religion. Laurie, like the author, is deep in an adulterous affair, torn by guilt and remorse but unable to give up her lover. 'Love', she says, 'kept me outside the Church . . . it drove like a hurricane, shattering everything in its way . . . the only thing was to go with it, because it always won.' But as Father Chantry Pigg warns her, there will be a price to pay: one day she will want to return to the Church, but it will be too late.

'Still the towers of Trebizond, the fabled city, shimmer on the far horizon, gated and walled and held in a luminous enchantment.' I saw the shimmering towers a few years ago – white blocks of flats smothering whatever remains of the last little bit of the Byzantine Empire Macaulay found so fascinating. I knew it wouldn't be the same even as she'd seen it in 1954 but I had a hopeful dream that some of the enchantment might have survived. I found a lively little Turkish port, short on magic, with a four-lane highway roaring between the town and the Black Sea where Jason and the Argonauts sailed and Xenophon's troops slept on the sand after their long march.

But, of course, I had to keep reminding myself that for Laurie – and Macaulay herself – Trebizond was not just a city, it was a metaphor for the Church she longed to re-enter but couldn't. 'That strange bright city on the hill, barred by its high gates . . . barred from all who do not desire to enter it more strongly than they desire all other cities.'

*

Rose Macaulay was born in 1881 into a clever, intellectual high Anglican family (Lord Macaulay the historian was a great-uncle). Her father, a teacher, had married his second cousin; they had seven children, and moved to the Italian coast for her mother's health. It was an idyllic childhood. The children, boys and girls alike, ran wild in glorious, sun-soaked, barefoot isolation. Rose was a late developer – even in her teens she still dreamed of becoming a sea captain. As an undergraduate at Oxford she was shy yet garrulous, an anorexic scholar who left without a degree after having had a nervous breakdown.

Returning home as a dutiful daughter, she started to write. There she might have stayed, but the First World War gave her the impetus to volunteer in a London hospital. She was a hopeless nurse who couldn't even scrub floors efficiently. Fortunately, in 1918 she found herself in the new Ministry of Information, writing Italian propaganda for the war effort. Here, at 36, she finally grew up, and fell in love with her boss, Gerald O'Donovan, an Irish ex-Roman Catholic priest and writer, married with three children. Their affair lasted for twenty years and had to be kept entirely secret – not easy in the gossipy London literary world they both inhabited.

Macaulay had a great gift for friendship. A rare combination of sharp wit, generosity of spirit and kindness made her many friends. Tall, skinny and neat as a furled umbrella, she knew everyone in the literary world from Rupert Brooke to Laurie Lee via Gilbert Murray, E. M. Forster, Isherwood and Auden, and Patrick Leigh Fermor. Virginia Woolf – who could never resist a bitchy put-down of a rival who at that time was more successful than she was – called her a faded beauty, so badly dressed, and added, 'Poor dear Rose, judging by her works, is a Eunuch.' She was wrong about that last jibe.

Macaulay made her name, and a living, by writing – novels, travel books, articles, reviews, even contributing to BBC radio arts pro-grammes. She was a famous party-goer, at every book launch, publishers' party and literary event, but at the same time was intensely secretive about her private life – and Gerald. For him she fell out with some of her family and left the Anglican Church which meant so much to her. She felt that in maintaining the affair she was com-mitting a mortal sin but she couldn't give him up. 'Adultery is a meanness and a stealing . . . a great selfishness and surrounded by lies lest it should be found out. And out of that meanness and selfishness and lying, flow love and joy and peace beyond anything that can be imagined,' says Laurie in Macaulay's voice.

In 1939 Macaulay was driving Gerald round Scotland. Driving with her was always perilous – everyone agreed she was a lovely per-son and a terrible driver. There was a crash and Gerald suffered serious head injuries. Three years later he died, from cancer, not from his injuries, but Macaulay felt intensely guilty. She wrote in an anon-ymous obituary for *The Times*: 'As a friend he never failed; his wise judgement and unstinting interest were always on tap behind . . . the sometimes sardonic wit that was his Irish heritage. To know him was to love him.'

That love stayed a secret until after Macaulay's own death in 1958.

She had gone back to the Church and her sister published a series of letters she had written to her Anglican confessor, revealing that her affair with Gerald was the reason she had stayed outside for so long. Her friends were incredulous. Evelyn Waugh (a ferocious Roman Catholic) wrote to Nancy Mitford, 'I thought her sharp but ladylike. Not at all the sort of person to gush to a parson.' And to Graham Greene (another RC), 'I always thought of her as the last spinster. Do you think her adultery was an hallucination?'

How much of *The Towers of Trebizond* is autobiographical?  Macaulay said she had put a lot of herself into it, and the tension between Laurie's love, guilt, remorse and an anguished loss of faith mirrors her own. 'Never was a novel (by me) more passionately in earnest . . . but perhaps I made too many jokes that confused people.' One joke of course is the famous opening line: 'Take my camel, dear, said Aunt Dot as she climbed down from this animal on her return from high Mass.' One confused review was headlined 'Mad camel plays big part in unusual book'.

There may be jokes at the beginning but the story becomes dark and sombre. It hinges round a fatal car crash. Laurie actually kills Vere on the way home from a furtive holiday, running into a bus that has jumped the lights. I don't know why Macaulay rewrote her less deadly accident with Gerald in this way. Perhaps it was a cathartic process for dealing with her guilt or perhaps she had ceased to grieve and the event had become grist to her novelist's mill. As far as I know, no one ever asked her.

At the end of the book Macaulay puts Laurie in the same position she herself was in when Gerald died. Their lovers are dead, the way back to the Church open. Macaulay did return but Laurie doesn't, feeling that to creep back when it was easy would devalue the intense happiness of her love for Vere. But there is still a price to be paid.

> When the years have all passed there will gape the uncomfortable and unpredictable dark void of death, and into this I shall at last fall headlong, down and down and down, and the prospect of that fall, that uprooting, that rending apart of body and spirit, that taking off into so blank an unknown, drowns me in mortal fear. Still the towers of Trebizond, the fabled city, shimmer on a far horizon, gated and walled . . . and I stand outside it, expelled in mortal grief.

I always hope when I reach this sombre ending that dear, adventurous, witty and kindly Rose did not herself feel such despair. She had such zest for living. In Laurie's words,

> After all, life for all its agonies of despair and loss and guilt, is exciting and beautiful, amusing and artful and endearing, full of liking and love, at times a poem, and a high adventure, at times noble and at times very gay; and whatever (if anything) is to come after it, we shall not have this life again.

AMANDA THEUNISSEN believes with Rose Macaulay that travel is the chief aim of Man but has a more mundane approach, thinking decent plumbing beats camping with a camel every time.

# All's Well that Ends Well

JIM RING

Children, as any parent will tell you, are innocent beings whose sensibilities it is the first duty of every parent to protect. They are sensitive, impressionable marshmallows, easily swayed, all too often led astray. St Ignatius of Loyola warns us that if he is given the child he will mould the man; Lenin likewise cautions, 'Give us the child for eight years [or, according to some sources, four] and it will be a Bolshevik forever.' As thunder tails lightning, it follows that the greatest care must be taken when giving children anything to read.

I can vouch for this as a parent myself; also as someone whose children grew up in the deep shadow cast by Harry Potter. I was more fortunate. Well before the age of reason I was drip-fed Edward Lear, Lewis Carroll, Richmal Crompton, Anthony Buckeridge, C. S. Lewis and, above all, Arthur Ransome and his Swallows and Amazons series.

Born in 1884, Ransome was the eldest son of a Leeds academic. He sought fame and fortune as a writer in Edwardian London and achieved notoriety when he was accused of libelling Lord Alfred Douglas in his 1912 biography of Oscar Wilde. He eventually made his name as a *Manchester Guardian* journalist covering the Russian Revolution, when he also eloped with Trotsky's secretary Evgenia Petrovna Shelepina, whom he would marry. Eventually returning to England, he refused a permanent post as the *Guardian's* foreign correspondent, determined to make his way as a children's novelist.

The Swallows and Amazons books were something of a novelty in

---

Arthur Ransome's *Coot Club* (1934) and *The Big Six* (1940) are both available in paperback from Red Fox at £7.99 each.

focusing on children's outdoor holiday adventures; they celebrated Ransome's own love of sailing with a level of knowledge and detail that was unprecedented; and their exemplary narratives reflected the author's extensive study of New World and Continental, as well as English, storytelling. Yet of the twelve books published between 1930 and 1948, it is for the five set in the English Lake District that Ransome is best remembered. The two tall tales *Peter Duck* and *Missee Lee*, the East Coast novels (*Secret Water* and *We Didn't Mean to Go to Sea*) and the coda *Great Northern?* are less celebrated, as are the pair set on the Norfolk Broads: *Coot Club* (1934) and its sequel *The Big Six* (1940). This is a pity.

Some of the best English writers have taken their inspiration from our meadows, coppices and hedgerows, our downs, uplands and wetlands, our coloured counties and blue remembered hills. Ransome stands high among them. 'If you know a bit of country really well,' he wrote, 'it takes a very active part in the making of your book. You can count on it. It is always there and, somehow or other, life flows from it into your story.'

The landscape of the lakes, where Ransome was schooled and where he lived for much of his adult life, certainly infuses the first book of the series. *Swallows and Amazons* (1930) features the Walker and Blackett children, the title taken from their sailing dinghies, the vividly rendered setting an amalgam of the lakes of Windermere and Coniston. The peak in Darien, the Amazon River and Wild Cat Island are as much a part of the story as the master of revels, the tomboy Nancy Blackett. Much the same can be said of the sequels *Swallowdale* (1931) and *Winter Holiday* (1933). In the second of these Ransome brilliantly evoked the Great Frost of 1895 that saw Windermere frozen from end to end.

There was the lake, and the moonlight pouring down on the white hills on the farther side. And there, out in the bay, lay the *Fram*, dark and motionless, frozen in the Arctic ice.

In *Winter Holiday*, Ransome also introduced two new characters, the metropolitan outsiders Dorothea Callum and her brother Dick. The one is a novelist manqué, the other a budding Einstein – though that makes them sound far stuffier than the thoroughly endearing pair they are.

In *Coot Club* he gives the Callums an adventure of their own on the Norfolk Broads. A splendid story it is too, springing from their need to acquire the sailing skills necessary to keep up with their new Lake District friends. Like the lake books, though, *Coot Club* is also a celebration of a corner of England to which Ransome moved in 1935 and which he came to love. Not far from his home on Suffolk's Shotley peninsula lie the reedy meres and meandering rivers of the Broads, a sprawling marshland drained by picturesque wind-pumps and graced by white-sailed yachts and great black-sailed trading wherries. Indeed, the book is structured virtually as a guidebook to the web of lakes that sprang from medieval peat diggings.

The club in the book's title brings together some of the young inhabitants of the Broads village of Horning in the common purpose of protecting coots – small black water birds – from their human predators. Among these latter is an older boy, George  Owdon. When a pair of nesting coots is disturbed by noisy holiday-makers in a motorboat (the 'Hullabaloos'), the oldest member of the Coot Club is driven to cast off their craft. This is Tom Dudgeon, the Horning doctor's son with whom Dick and Dorothea have made friends. Tom and the Farland twins (nicknamed Port and Starboard) are persuaded by the Callums' host Mrs Barrable to teach her guests to sail in her yacht, *Teasel*. Tom, the twins, the Callums, Mrs Barrable and her pug William are then chased all over the Broads by the vindictive Hullabaloos, while Owdon acts as their informant on the *Teasel*'s whereabouts.

'What can be devised by way of Triumph, to be achieved by effort and so to provide the happy ending that must almost to the end look

as if it can't come off?' That was the question posed by Ransome to Margaret and Charles Renold, from whom he sometimes sought literary advice and to whom he later dedicated *The Big Six*. I will not spoil your enjoyment by revealing the denouement, but instrumental to it are three extras – the Horning boatbuilders' sons, Joe, Bill and Pete, who vacillate between playful piracy, bird protection and boat salvage, and who take their collective name from their pirate vessel, an old ship's lifeboat, the *Death and Glory*.

*Coot Club* was followed by *Pigeon Post* (1936), in which Ransome returned to the Lake District to evoke a summer drought with all the skill with which he had depicted the winter fells. Blacketts, Walkers and Callums turn gold prospectors. This was the very first winner of the Carnegie Medal, the UK's oldest and most prestigious award for children's writing. *We Didn't Mean to Go to Sea* followed in 1937, thought by some to be Ransome's masterpiece, though for me compromised by the absence of the Blacketts. *Secret Water* came in 1939, set on the Walton backwaters in Essex.

Casting around for a new subject, a sequel to *Coot Club* seemed a natural progression. Ransome appears to have owed the idea of a detective story to Margaret Renold. This was the golden age of detective fiction, and Ransome was a devotee of the genre. He at once recognized that the established cast of the original Broads novel could readily turn their hands to new roles. To the Renolds he wrote:

Detective. Why not? Now then. George Owdon of *Coot Club* is obviously the right criminal. Tom and the Death and Glories are the right detectives, with the help of Dorothea's imagination and Dick's scientific mind. NOW, I see it this way. It would be all wrong for the detectives to snoop out of public spirit with the hope of handing George over to justice. The detective work must be forced upon them TO CLEAR THEMSELVES of some villainy of which, thanks to George Owdon, they are bearing the blame. What the devil can it be?

The plot Ransome developed was a logical extension of the events of *Coot Club*. The Coots, with their president's record of casting off boats, would be the first port of call for the authorities should other boats be loosed. So reason George Owdon and his accomplice Ralph Strakey. The pair embark on a campaign of vandalism, casting off boats in Horning itself and in two nearby villages, Ranworth and Potter Heigham. Constable Tedder and the public duly rise to the bait and fall on Joe, Pete and Bill, the Death and Glories.

At this point Dick and Dorothea arrive on their holiday. At once rejecting suggestions that any of the Coots could be guilty, and despairing of any help from Constable Tedder, they turn detective. The Coot Club shed in the Dudgeons' garden becomes Scotland Yard, and the Big Six is born.

'But who are the Big Six?' asked Pete.

'It's the big five really,' said Dorothea. 'They are the greatest detectives in the world. They sit in their cubby-holes in Scotland Yard and solve one mystery after another.'

'But why Six?'

'There are only five of them and there are six of us,' said Dorothea.

The story uses some of the standard ploys of detective fiction: the scattering of clues, the laying of false trails, the stoking of moral outrage against the innocent unjustly accused, and the raising of stakes as a second crime (the theft of boat shackles) is committed. But it is elevated above the generic by Ransome's tireless integration of the storyline with his characters' lives. Mrs Barrable's pug is recast as a bloodhound, the *Death and Glory*'s chimney becomes a vital piece of evidence, Dick's tyro skills as a photographer are turned to police work. There's also an ingenious sub-plot about the catching of a huge pike, a feat which provides the indigent Death and Glories with unexplained wealth, which Constable Tedder attributes to the sale of the stolen shackles. Ransome gives Dorothea the role of leading detective, allowing her to develop her forensic skills and to put herself in the perpetrators' shoes. Finally, there is a masterly climax.

Owdon and Strakey, fearful that the evidence has yet to clinch the guilt of the Death and Glories, are tempted into Dorothea's trap to cast off one last boat before the hands of the law close on the Coots' collars. On the eve of their formal interview with the local solicitor – Port and Starboard's father Mr Farland – the Big Six take their turn to stake out the *Cachalot*. Hiding in Horning's riverside bushes, they plan to take by flashlight a photograph of the criminals casting off the boat. The criminals take the bait. Whether or not the photograph – taken by debutant photographer Pete – has come out and will disclose the miscreants' identity is withheld until three chapters later.

With great ingenuity Ransome conjures up 'the happy ending that must almost to the end look as if it can't come off'. Mr Farland dismisses as circumstantial the considerable evidence of Owdon's guilt that the Big Six have amassed. Enter stage left Constable Tedder, in the company of Strakey and Owdon. They witnessed, they say, Bill casting off the *Cachalot*. 'Open and shut,' says Tedder. 'We know who done it now.' Enter stage right Dick and Pete, bearing a photographic printing frame. Several more nerve-racking moments pass before the photograph is sufficiently developed to be handed to Mr Farland.

'A very remarkable likeness,' said Mr Farland. 'What do you think, constable?'

Mr Tedder looked at the photograph.

'Well I'll be danged!' he said.

Mr Farland thought for some minutes.

'The value of evidence', he said, 'fluctuates with its context . . .

This photograph will in any court of law (here he looked gravely at George and his friend) serve as proof that the boat was cast off by George Owdon and . . .'

'Strakey,' said Mr Tedder.

So Ransome spins on a sixpence, the tables are turned, the guilty are identified, the innocent are vindicated, and justice is done.

*The Big Six* is a superb detective story and demonstrates not only Ransome's determination never to repeat himself but also his ability to develop still further the heartening theme of children's ability to rise to life's occasions. It provides an indelible portrait of the Norfolk Broads between the wars. It is a book with a crystalline moral purpose. It is, all in all, an irreplaceable contribution to his Arcadian world.

And much of this is more than can be said for some of the books I have been obliged to read aloud from time to time. This is worth parents bearing in mind, particularly if they wish to provide the happy ending to their children's adolescence that almost to the end looks as if it can't come off. My wife and I managed to leaven our daughter and son's diet of less desirable literature with a fair dose of Ransome. The result was that they turned out all right, in the end.

JIM RING is a writer and film-maker, the father of two and husband of one.

# An American Childhood

MARKIE ROBSON-SCOTT

*Childsplay* was published in 1961. It was Eda Lord's first novel, though now it would probably be called a memoir, and is an account of her childhood (the first-person narrator is unnamed), starting in 1911 when she was 4 and ending in 1917. The first and last chapters are set in Evanston, Illinois, where Eda's formidable, regal grandmother lived; the rest takes place in the wilds of Missouri, Oklahoma and Tennessee.

Eda was born in Durango, Mexico, where her father owned silver mines, and they – Eda, her father, her stepbrother Jimmy and her part-Cherokee stepmother Motheranne – were constantly on the move from one mining venture to another. 'Moving every year made it natural for me to reckon not by when but where,' she wrote. 'My past was a geography and happened in places like layers in a cake . . .'

I was 11 when I first read *Childsplay*. Its urbane, spare style and the atmosphere it created – even the typeface in our Simon and Schuster edition was exotically American and the title had a lower-case c – were irresistible, so different from my sheltered London life in the 1950s and '60s. (A reviewer said, 'Here is a writer who uses language as if it had just been invented . . . no self-pity, no sentimentality, no vulgarity.') Eda and her partner Sybille Bedford were regular visitors to my parents' flat in Marylebone, for Eda and my father had known each other in Paris and Berlin in the 1930s.

Sybille was less appealing to me. She was preoccupied with import-

---

Eda Lord, *Childsplay* (1961), is out of print but we can obtain second-hand copies.

ant things and spoke fast and nervily. She was very fair with weak eyes and wore a green sun visor and dull men's clothes. Reading *Childsplay*, however, added layers to my fondness for elegant Eda, who was more fun. She had a soft face, deeply lined, and a husky American voice, and she smoked a lot. In an armchair in our sitting-room, her long legs in dark stockings, she drank black Nescafé from a thermos provided by my mother. Later I found out she was an alcoholic and needed coffee permanently on hand. In her fifties, she had an understated glamour. Her obituary in 1976 remarked that 'her high spirits and daring courage were matched by striking good looks and a magnificent physique'.

One of *Childsplay*'s strengths is the contrast between Eda's two lives: the cold, well-ordered one with her grandmother, whose hobby is designing houses and whose attention to detail in running her own is 'as persistent as a dentist's drill. Cooks and housemaids never lasted the month,' and the freedom of life with her pioneering father, Jimmy and Motheranne.

Jimmy, a year older than Eda, is more of a friend than a brother, something that as an only child I found fascinating, and both of them are good at fighting – never more than was strictly necessary, 'but we had quite a steady grind of it. Each time we changed schools, we would have to re-establish ourselves all over again.' They invent a sophisticated naval warfare game with a poker-based scoring method that obsesses them both and that alleviates the boredom of first grade for Eda, who's already well ahead of the others in her class thanks to a tutor she had in Evanston. None of the other children at school have any idea about poker, and the boys are only interested in foot-ball. But Jimmy and Eda are coolly self-sufficient: they go to the circus and movies together and travel alone on trains, sometimes getting lost.

Life can be harsh. Their father often spanks them, 'quickly and efficiently', as does an unpleasant housekeeper known as Wigwam. And when Lilly-Mae, the maid, smothers her crying baby (Eda, looking through the keyhole, witnesses this), Motheranne explains that as the baby girl didn't have a father, Lilly-Mae felt she couldn't afford to keep her because girls 'gave no promise of a return' – they couldn't earn money as easily as boys. Eda decides that keeping up with Jimmy, with his Morse Code, dry batteries and copper coils, is of prime importance for her future. Perhaps she can be a wireless operator on a ship.

At the age of 8 or so, Eda embarks on a series of excursions in Joplin, Missouri, crisscrossing the city by herself, having stolen Motheranne's streetcar tickets and lied about where she's going after school. I identified strongly with her deviousness and independence, although my mother or nanny came with me on the No. 74 bus from Baker Street to and from school in South Kensington. I tried coming home alone once when I was about 10, but I missed the appointed bus and my mother, waiting at the bus stop, became hysterical. Eda's parents were often away and then Wigwam looked after the children, taking them to a morgue as a punishment when they're in the Wild West mining-town of Okmulgee, Oklahoma, where battles rage at school between American Indians and whites. 'With the coming of spring, the air became filled with stones.' Eda is knocked out and gets a goose-egg sized bump, but no one takes much notice.

In Embreeville, Tennessee, where some of the backwoods people think the Civil War is still on, her father teaches them to fire a Colt .45 and Eda gets the hang of it quicker than Jimmy because she cuts corners on shooting style. 'Could it be that which made the awful difference between boys and girls? That boys stick to rules?' Reading about that prompted me to go to the toyshop with my nanny and spend my pocket money on a cap gun. My parents didn't say much, but their disapproval was so evident that I gave it to a boy up the road a day or so later.

In Embreeville Eda's father discovers surface coal in abundance and plans to shoot the mountainside with water cannon to extract it. Waiting for the cannon to arrive, they live a life of luxury in a country club, where East Coast mining experts and their wives stroll over the lawns. The wives, thinks Eda, are like birds of paradise, but although they chatter all the time and take her to their bedrooms to show her their cloud-like dresses and face-creams, they're tough and reckless underneath. 'If I must be a woman when I grow up, I thought I'd rather be a bird than anything . . . I would live in a club like this and swim all day long.'

When America enters the war in 1917 everything changes. Her beloved father dies suddenly when working in shipbuilding out east and 10-year-old Eda is forced to make a terrible choice. If she decides to go with Jimmy and Motheranne, says her grandmother, she'll never see her, or any of her father's family, again. As Jimmy will be sent away to school and she knows Motheranne's opinion of father-less children, she plumps for her grandmother. She might be cold, 'but at least you knew where you stood with her'. The cruelty of this stunned me – I couldn't imagine her life without Jimmy.

Eda's next novel, *A Matter of Choosing* (1963), takes up her story as a young woman in California; the third, *Extenuating Circumstances* (1971), is loosely based on her experiences of living through the Second World War in the south of France (she was interned by the Germans for a time as an enemy alien).

In 2006, years after my father died, I found piles of confiding letters from Eda to him. In 1934 she was living in Paris, having left the USA in 1931 after a short, disastrous marriage. My father was then in Berlin, where they'd met, both of them part of a circle that in-cluded Christopher Isherwood. In Paris, Eda was living with another mutual friend, the physical therapist Tania Kurella, a Polish-German refugee who'd left Berlin in 1933.

Once again Eda was being forced to choose, this time between two lovers – Tania and Joan Black, a wealthy socialite and friend of Nancy Cunard, who sounds like one of those birds of paradise. 'It's hell, you know,' Eda wrote. 'I still don't know how I can leave Tania . . . Memories of our lives together are so sweet it's like thrusting knives into myself.' But falling for Joan was 'like a crack of lightning open-ing an abyss'. After being given an ultimatum by both women and agonizing for months, she chose Joan. Tania married the writer Jimmy Stern.

Just after the war, Tania wrote to my father from Fire Island, New York, 'the queerest place I have ever known'. She and Jimmy had spent the war in the USA, and were close friends of W. H. Auden; in fact they'd bought a tiny Fire Island cottage with him. She'd managed to keep in touch with Eda who, she said, had given up drink, 'a ter-rific achievement' (it didn't last). She is longing to see Eda again, but not Joan Black, a 'limited and domineering character' who, she says, forced Eda to stay in France during the war against her will. But, thinks Tania, 'Eda might one day write a good book about it all.' She wrote three, each one a wonderful picture of an era. But *Childsplay* is her masterpiece.

MARKIE ROBSON-SCOTT is a freelance writer who has worked on many magazines and newspapers including *Harpers & Queen*, *Vogue* and the *Guardian*. She finds that the letters written to her father by his friends in the 1930s are a continuing source of surprise and fascination.

# England, Their England

### JONATHAN KEATES

Daniel Macklin

At the time of writing, the town of Tewkesbury, in the north-west corner of Gloucestershire, has been cut off by the flooding of its four rivers: the Severn and Avon, at whose confluence it stands, and smaller streams named Swilgate and Carrant. Only the great Norman abbey, with its necklace of Gothic chapels, rises above the turbid brown tides that surge across the meadows. England is more richly watered than elsewhere in northern Europe, but now this very same element seems thoroughly hostile to the humans who planted the woods, ploughed the fields and staked the hedges enclosing them.

This sense of nature reasserting herself would have appealed to Tewkesbury's greatest writer. I'm not talking about Dinah Maria Mulock, author, as Mrs Craik, of the once-popular *John Halifax Gentleman* (1856), or of Henry Yorke, scion of the local gentry, who wrote under the pen-name Henry Green. The talent I'd like to celebrate is less blatantly moralizing than Craik's and not quite so aesthetically self-conscious as Green's. A Tewkesburian middle ground between them belongs firmly to John Moore, whose best books are rooted, as theirs for whatever reason are not, in the changing rural scene around him. Moore's passionate absorption is understandable. It's hard not to see this area of England, where the three counties of Worcestershire, Herefordshire and Gloucestershire converge, as enchanted ground, the more so for me since I grew up there. My

---

John Moore, *The Waters under the Earth* (1965), is out of print but we can obtain second-hand copies.

remembered hills are the pink granite Malverns and my land of lost content is that rolling terrain of pastures, cornlands and orchards stretching eastwards to Bredon and south to the Severn estuary.

Moore was, in whatever sense, all over this country. His family's auctioneering business, based in Tewkesbury, sold the livestock, harvests and machinery of local farmers. He knew about heifers, steers and store cattle, the difference between a wether and a tup, and just how a Fordson Major compared with a Massey Harris when trundling a combine. He went shooting, fished the streams and, as his friends recalled, maintained more than a nodding acquaintance with various poachers across the big estates. His amazing eye for detail in the habits of wild creatures, the rhythm of the seasons and the texture of the landscape made Moore a classic example of the 'man who used to notice such things' celebrated in Hardy's poem 'Afterwards'.

A prolific writer on the English countryside, Moore never sentimentalized his subject, fully understanding what was pitiless, violent and unpredictable within it and familiar with the surly resentments, fatalism, ignorance and superstition darkening rural life. Sensitive to its poetic inspirations, like Edward Thomas whose work he helped to bring back into favour, Moore was just as close to Richard Jefferies, that pioneer rustic realist, in striking the perfect balance of fluency and detachment so as to give authority to his writing as a countryman.

Moore's energy in this cause was the more focused for his sense of the rapid, often brutal changes taking place in the agricultural scene around him. His particular patch of England may have seemed very much an *Angleterre profonde* of meadows, hedgerows, thatched cottages and mossy churchyards, but hostile forces were poised to undermine its traditional fabric. In his splendid Brensham trilogy, begun in 1946 (and recently reissued by Slightly Foxed), he had bidden an elegantly crafted farewell to the Tewkesbury vale of his youth and to several of its more colourful characters. His last major work, however, *The Waters under the Earth* (1965), uses the novel form to engage more intensely with themes of survival, resistance and compromise in a world where, as the book's most anguished protagonist declares at its opening, 'Nothing's going to be the same again, ever.'

It is the 1950s and we are once again in Moore country, at Doddington Manor, not far from Elmbury (Tewkesbury), where the Seldons have been squires since Domesday. Things are not quite what they were at the manor house. It has crooked chimneys, cracked roof tiles and rot both wet and dry in its beams and floors, fashioned from the great oaks in the park planted by Ferdinando ('Ferdo') Seldon's ancestors. The oaks themselves are menaced now by the intrusion of a new road sweeping remorselessly across the river near the ancient ferry and chomping up two woods named Trafalgar and Waterloo. 'Could the Powers that Be really do such things upon a man's land nowadays?' Ferdo wonders. 'Of course they could, for that was the way the weather was, that was the way the tide was running.'

His wife Janet sees things altogether differently. In *The Waters under the Earth* she emerges as one of the most compelling figures for her refusal to make peace with the era in which she has the bad luck to live. Since this is a novel which painstakingly examines the nature of Englishness for good or ill, class forms a significant element in the story and Janet Seldon's social prejudices and presumptions as 'her ladyship', the squire's wife, are sustained with a doggedness that assumes an increasingly pathetic desperation. Moore neither condemns nor mocks her for this, choosing instead to use extracts from her diary, with its underlinings, words in capitals and schoolroom French, to provide an alternative thread throughout the narrative.

Ferdo and Janet have one child, Susan, who is not the *Country Life* girls-in-pearls daughter such parents might wish for. 'I'm frightened for you sometimes,' says a friend, 'I've got a feeling that you – attract the lightning, my dear.'

In this guise she makes a memorable heroine, courting accident yet always enduring its scars. When, at the Stow-on-the-Wold horse fair, evoked by the writer with anthropological gusto, Susan buys a 'ribby, rakish' mare named Nightshade, the beast perfectly matches her new owner, 'cantering delightfully on the razor edge of fear'.

A gift for staying metaphorically in the saddle is what Susan has inherited from her father. While Janet, in the pages of her diary, laments 'the palmy days' when the 'whole county ORGANIZED for hunting', Ferdo adopts a far more speculative and philosophical attitude to the encroaching present. He enjoys arguing with Susan's friend Stephen Le Mesurier, the local Tory candidate in the forthcoming General Election, whose Conservatism is suspect to Janet because he is too clever by half, and that half happens to be Jewish. Equally Ferdo relishes a chance to spar with the boorish nouveau riche Colonel Daglingworth, whose local business interests are unlikely to be thwarted by qualms over heritage, tradition and wild nature. For Ferdo, a wartime naval officer, however, contrariness of all kinds needs to be met with equanimity, summarized in his mantra, '*Pro bono publico*, no bloody panico'.

The Seldons will need such equanimity in spades when Fenton, the new gardener, arrives with his wife and five children. 'We've no real reason to imagine he's a Communist or anything of the kind,' Ferdo assures a fretful Janet, but she requires a good deal more persuasion after meeting Mrs Fenton, 'one of those angular, waspish, red-haired, hygienic, purposive women with spectacles, who look intellectual even if they aren't'. The truth is that the gardener's wife, while being Lady Seldon's polar opposite, is also her mirror image. Each woman, whatever their difference in status, matches the other in a tyrannical absence of vision or imagination.

On one of its many levels, *The Waters under the Earth* is a worthy enough rival to E. M. Forster's *Howards End* in asking 'Who will inherit England?' The Seldons and the Fentons may not be as sophisticated in their fashioning as the Schlegels and the Wilcoxes, but they are just as authentic and the underlying question remains the same. Moore's plot is in any case staked out along the wider historical trajectory of post-war Britain. Susan's first fiancé, her cousin Tony, heir to Ferdo's baronetcy, is taken prisoner while serving in Korea, young Ben Fenton is called up to fight in the Suez affair, and a Coronation Day fête is a freezing non-event.

The drama of surviving the muddle, bewilderment and despair threatening to overwhelm Doddington is heightened by Moore's neat deployment of symbols. As Ferdo learns, eventually, to welcome the grey squirrels who have driven out their red cousins represented on his family escutcheon, he is listening, at the same time, to the motorway engineers felling the great oaks in his park. Honey fungus, gross intruder, the woodland equivalent of Colonel Daglingworth, is spreading decay among the coppices even as the subterranean waters of the novel's title are starting to flood the manor-house cellars. Stephen Le Mesurier sees the rising streams as emblematic of something deeper, an ebb and flow in the currents of English perpetuity. 'Powerful, ubiquitous, secret, they would burst out of confinement', buoying up some and drowning others.

Janet appears a destined casualty of this hidden tide. The novel brims with cleverly engineered episodes in which essential narrative strides dovetail with Moore's appetite for scene-painting. Daglingworth's pheasant shoot is one such, Susan's triumphant point-to-point gallop on Nightshade is another, but best of them all, for its ominous terseness, is the Women's Institute AGM at which Janet, having deluded herself that she will be president for life, is cruelly ousted by the wife of a local factory owner. That evening's diary entry is among the bitterest. 'Beasts!! BEASTS!!! Can hardly believe it after all these yrs. Know I wasn't v. good, not my métier, but did my best and LOVED it (Why???) Why do I mind??? Could not easily say Despise myself S-pity most horrible.'

Deference swiftly fades among Elmbury shopkeepers, and teddy boys rough up Janet's old hunter, while Susan's own alter ego, Doddington's maid Rosemary, becomes pregnant and is forced into a hasty marriage with her lowlife village boyfriend before running off to a job in Birmingham in return for servicing the lecherous

Daglingworth. The world, as Susan and Ferdo come to understand, has to be reckoned with on its own highly ambiguous terms. Father and daughter are ready to negotiate, as neither Janet nor Mrs Fenton seems capable of doing. Stephen Le Mesurier, meanwhile, seeks a bromide in the poetry of Hopkins and Baudelaire to deaden the coarse, inexorable foot-stomp of progress across the Gloucestershire Arcadia. Watching Fenton stacking a bonfire, Egbert the handyman recalls a superstitious rhyme:

> Make a fire of elder tree,
> Death within the house shall be.

Yet this very same death will also signal a kind of solution or release.

John Moore has been accused of sentimentalizing the book's ending, but this is to misunderstand his obvious intention in writing it. Yes, there is, thank goodness, a wonderful scatter, through its pages, of the author's country lore – the colour of a beech tree bole, the song of a chiffchaff, 'a sky that faded from primrose to a starling's-egg blue' – but this never muffles or clutters the narrative's overall integrity. The modern demand for conclusions of unmitigated bleakness and misery now has its own musty banality. There's enough anyway, at the close of *The Waters under the Earth*, to satisfy this kind of cliché. Doddington Manor will tumble down, damaged cousin Tony will inherit the estate, Ben Fenton's Suez wound may yet turn septic and Susan's baby by him may be stillborn. This is to miss the point entirely. What survives, in Moore's England, is its atavistic capacity for shape-shifting and self-renewal, with a little help from Ferdo's '*Pro bono publico*, no bloody panico', Fenton's bonfires and the occasional no-confidence vote at the WI.

JONATHAN KEATES grew up not far from Tewkesbury and his first published book, *The Companion Guide to the Shakespeare Country*, included chapters on many places familiar to John Moore.

# Unravelling Burushaski

LESLEY DOWNER

When I was young I thought I knew exactly where the real Shangri-La was. It was the land of Hunza, in north-west Pakistan, or if not, then Gilgit or Chitral, and those magical names remained with me as I grew up.

Years later I was clearing out my father's things and discovered a worn, spineless, much-used book on his shelves. It was called *Language Hunting in the Karakorum*. More years passed before I discovered where and what the Karakorum are and where my identification of Hunza with Shangri-La had come from. My father never went there but this book must have convinced him that Hunza was that perfect, unspoilt place, and it became one of those certainties that he passed on to me. I settled down to read it. With that rather forbidding title, I hadn't been expecting such a thrilling tale of travel and adventure, every bit as gripping and informative and exciting as the best travel books.

*Language Hunting in the Karakorum* (1939) was written by E. O. (Emily Overend) Lorimer, wife of Lieutenant-Colonel David 'DL' Lorimer, who had been posted to Gilgit as Political Officer in 1920 to advise its ruler, the Mir, and effectively be the real power right across this British-held territory. Asked by DL's superior officer whether she would be willing to go with her husband to the hardship posting of Gilgit, Emily replied, 'I'm willing to go with my husband to HELL.'

---

E. O. Lorimer, *Language Hunting in the Karakorum* (1939), is out of print but we can obtain second-hand copies.

After four years DL and Emily retired to England, having spent most of their spare time in Gilgit getting to grips with the Shina language, and most especially Burushaski, the fiendishly difficult Hunza language that belongs to no known family of languages. In 1934, now in their mid-fifties, they decided to return under their own steam so that DL could continue his study of Burushaski. *Language Hunting in the Karakorum* is Emily's fascinating account of their year and a quarter in Hunza, their adventures, experiences and the many people whom they befriended. It's an extraordinary story and winningly written, elegant, witty, self-deprecating and humorous.

The first hurdle was to get there. They sailed by ship to Bombay, then drove to Srinagar in Kashmir. From there the only way onwards was by pony. Assured by telegraph that the snow had cleared from the high passes, they were well on their way when they discovered that their informant was wrong. The passes were still deep in snow. With summer approaching the only option was to travel through the night when the snow froze and so was sufficiently hard for the ponies to walk on.

Lorimer describes their hair-raising journey through sometimes impenetrable darkness along narrow mountain tracks, clinging to the pony's mane and bracing herself on the stirrups as it struggled up and down near-vertical slopes, or skipping across moving rock falls when the ponies refused to carry them along particularly treacherous terrain.

If you could sail down on a tea tray it would not be more than three miles to river level, but the graded road is full ten miles, now interminably crisscrossing the steep face of the Hattu Pir where it seems impossible that a road should cling (and in fact it often slithers quietly downhill and has to be coaxed into place again), now along a rock-shelf where the left cliff almost over-hangs the track and the right falls sheer 800 feet into the river below.

Eventually, after a brief stopover in their old home in Gilgit, they arrive in Hunza where they settle into a bungalow in the small fort-village of Aliabad. While DL takes on informants to help him unravel Burushaski's enormously complex grammar and record Hunza folklore and history, Emily is out and about. Having already spent four years in the region and having acquired a fair smattering of Burushaski herself, she is able to make friends and is soon a sympathetic and eager participant in village life. The Hunzukuts, as they are called, address her in terms which she translates as 'Mother dear'.

She chips in with the daily work, trying her hand at threshing and sorting, spinning and weaving, noting down vocabulary and inspiring gales of affectionate laughter when she gets words wrong. The Hunzukuts are amazed at her inability to perform the simplest tasks, such as spinning, and they tease her when she fails to tell a diseased ear of millet from a healthy one or when she worries about children with babies on their backs falling off the precipitous walls which form some of the main walkways in this mountainous terrain.

Emily for her part is constantly impressed with their cheeriness and the perfection with which they carry out their daily tasks – bridges built without scientific instruments of any sort, yet completely straight, stable, reliable and long-lasting. In many ways their lifestyle is an improvement on hers, she finds, from her shoes which make it difficult to clamber around the steep terraces, to her reliance on chairs which means she finds it uncomfortable to sit on the ground.

When she's invited to visit neighbours' homes, she checks on the proper compliments to make and the gifts to bring, not so valuable as to embarrass but that will be appreciated and be of use. She describes the square stone houses where the men sleep on a wide bench along one side and the women along a bench on the other. There is usually a cow in a byre in front, and most gardens have apple trees, mulberries, peaches, apricots and vines.

She befriends the next-door neighbours – Grandfather, who built the house himself, 'my friend, Bibi Gimo', the *ruli gus* or housewife-in-chief, and Najat, the beautiful wife of the younger son, who has 'the happiest face I have ever seen, and a natural grace of bearing and manner that would adorn any station in any country'. Then there's Ustad Nadiro, a famous carpenter, weaver and bootmaker, and his wife, 'a sporting old lady . . . with a game leg and toothless gums, indefatigable energy, a priceless sense of humour and an unfailing smile'. In Hunza the women are strong, opinionated and respected and, though nominally Muslim, certainly don't cover their heads or faces.

There are wonderful photographs of many of the people whom we meet in these pages, at work or outside their houses, beaming glorious smiles. As Emily writes, 'There never was a people anywhere with such a gift for looking happy as the Hunzukuts.' There are photographs too of the spectacular mountain landscape amidst which these people live.

Emily also fills us in on historical events like the British conquest of Hunza, though she is, of course, of her time. An old man she meets who was part of the resistance to the British refers to 'the downfall of Hunza', though it was clearly not a 'downfall' in Emily's eyes. He shows off the sword and muzzle-loader which he used in the relief of Chitral five years later and talks with a tinge of unconcealed regret about the days when 'men were men and fighting was toward'.

Emily is aware of her privileged position. She is in the society but not of it. She will leave but the Hunzukuts are there for life, and when winter comes and everyone runs short of food, she and DL still have plenty. And of course she and DL have worked with and know the Mir well and so are treated as honoured guests. All the same, in the year and a quarter she spends in Hunza, her curiosity, warmth and command of the language enable her to delve deeply and sympathetically into the local society.

She and DL are the first Europeans ever to brave the ferociously harsh Hunza winter and enjoy the festivals that brighten the dark, dreary days. The Bopfau, the Barley Seed-Sowing, marks the end of winter in February. Invited by the Mir, they go by horse to Altit Fort, perched high on a cliff with the houses almost literally built on top of one another, surrounding a courtyard 'with no straight walls for edges'. Everyone is in their gayest and brightest dress. There is archery on horseback, music, clowning and splendid dancing. The following day the Mir, in a gold-embroidered velvet cloak and a silk turban, presides over the Seed-Sowing festival.

One chapter I found particularly fascinating. In it Emily describes how DL goes about learning a language no outsider has ever learnt before. Burushaski has no writing system, but it is an incredibly rich and complex language with different words for each stage and variety of crops, buds, fruits, fields, sheep and even baskets, and a fiendishly complicated grammar. Imagine being a non-French-speaker ship-wrecked off the coast of France, meeting only illiterate fishermen and trying to acquire spoken French, she writes. It's a daunting task.

I realized then why my father had used this book so much that the spine fell off. He spent years among the Yao and Miao hill tribes of Laos, unravelling their languages in just this way and assembling dictionaries. As I discovered for myself in Japan, language is the key to Looking-Glass Land. Unless you can speak it you'll always be the outsider looking in. Language enables you to step through into a different world.

And thus Emily takes us deep inside this world, getting under the skin of this rarefied place in the days when Political Officers were the only westerners who ever visited. Hunza was not really Shangri-La; life there was too hard to call it that. But it was a remarkable place, a lost horizon. *Language Hunting in the Karakorum* is a unique record of a world that no longer exists and the story of an extraordinarily rare experience. Today we can visit Hunza. But who, even today, speaks Burushaski?

LESLEY DOWNER is half Chinese but has spent much of her life in Japan, either in reality or imagination. She writes fiction and non-fiction on Japan, including four epic historical novels, The Shogun Quartet, based on fact and set in the mid-nineteenth century.

# The Joy of Sex

DEREK PARKER

In the late 1780s the librarian at the Bohemian castle of Dux, fifty miles from Prague, was trying to finish his autobiography. His employer, Count Joseph Karl von Waldstein, chamberlain to the Emperor, was an amiable man, but in his absence his jealous major-domo Feldkirchner made the librarian's life a misery. The servants disregarded his orders, the cook served him cold, inedible meals, dogs were encouraged to bark outside his room at night, and during the day a hunting horn with a peculiarly unpleasant tone was sounded at intervals. Everyone in the castle was encouraged to laugh at the elderly man's over-meticulous manners and old-fashioned dress. All in all, it was remarkable that Giacomo Casanova succeeded in completing his masterpiece – though despite its enormous length it still ends so abruptly that there might have been a few more pages to come.

*The Story of My Life* is arguably the most honest and self-revelatory autobiography ever written, and also a colourful and highly entertaining picture of eighteenth-century Europe. The detail is extraordinary – so vivid and immediate that one might doubt its accuracy. But apart from the fact that Casanova seems to have had almost perfect recall, throughout his life he left packets of notes containing his immediate impressions and reactions to events and personalities

Giacomo Casanova's *History of My Life* in Willard Trask's 6-volume translation is out of print, though copies of some volumes can be found second-hand. *The Complete Memoirs of Casanova: 'The Story of My Life'* is available in a single volume: Benediction Classics · Hb · 1,166pp · £49.99 · ISBN 9781781393796.

with friends dotted throughout Europe, which he collected for his project at Dux. So when he writes of social life in Venice or Fontainebleau, Vienna, Warsaw or Constantinople, St Petersburg or London, we can count on the detail being true to the life of the time; and when he records conversations with Catherine of Russia or Frederick of Prussia, Voltaire, Goethe, Mozart or Benjamin Franklin, it's with the help of notes made within a few hours of the event, so their voices can reliably be heard.

Casanova's autobiography in the great modern English translation by Willard Trask runs to 3,700 pages and 6 volumes, so to describe it as 'a book' might seem a touch disrespectful. It is really a great series of anecdotes, of almost cinematic scenes: adventurous, farcical, romantic, supernatural, erotic, disgraceful. He makes the most of them all.

Born in Venice and completely neglected by his actor parents, he was 9 when his grandmother packed him off to the University of Padua, which he left at 12 with a degree in clerical law. Back in Venice he spent the briefest possible time in a seminary, took minor orders, became an abbé (the least significant order of the Church) and acquired a rich Venetian senator, Matteo Bragadin, as a patron – until he was discovered in less than ecclesiastical discussion with the senator's mistress. Thrown out of the palazzo, he decided that the world would become his oyster. And so it did.

The escapade which made him famous throughout Europe was his escape from the Leads, the Venetian prison from which no prisoner had ever escaped before. He was thrown into it in 1755, when he was 30, condemned to five years' imprisonment for blasphemy and 'affront to decency' (both accusations, one has to say, amply justified). One night he and an accomplice broke out through the roof of the gaol to sit for a moment astride the ridge, looking down on the moonlit city, then lowered themselves on a rope made from torn sheets to crawl perilously along the broken, rotting gutter, smash through a window into the throne-room of the Doge's palace and stroll down the grand staircase to freedom. Little wonder that

Casanova dined out on the story all over Europe before making a small fortune from a published account.

His honesty as an autobiographer is underlined by the fact that he never hesitates to reveal himself as a lying, bragging, scamming rogue – for instance in his account of an incident at Mantua, where he met a foolish, rich gentleman farmer who boasted of possessing the dagger with which St Peter cut off the ear of the High Priest's servant at Gethsemane. Casanova assured him he could supply him with the sheath, which would greatly improve the relic's value. This he made from a piece of old leather, selling it to the farmer for a considerable sum before going on to scam the man further by promising to use occult spells, involving the man's own daughter, to reveal the whereabouts of buried treasure. (I'll spare readers the details, except to say that Casanova never hesitated to underline the fact that during occult experiments the presence of a naked virgin was obligatory.)

Avoiding, or perhaps just keeping quiet about, the erotic pages, historians have ransacked Casanova's autobiography for the details of eighteenth-century life he noted shakily down on odd pieces of paper as he bumped across Europe in frowsty, crowded coaches over dreadful roads. During his relatively short time in London he attended the highly fashionable assemblies given at Carlisle House by the society hostess Mrs Cornelys, formerly Teresa Imer, whom he had known years earlier in Venice (she had thrown her infant child out of bed in order to make room for him). Though society queued around Soho Square to attend these events, inside Carlisle House Casanova noted the 'promenades of scantily clad young women' which suggested that the assemblies were less sedate than the social columns suggested. He was received at court, where, though the King (George III) spoke in such a low voice that he could only reply with a polite bow, he flirted delightfully with Queen Charlotte, who was clearly taken with him.

It was in London that he reached the low point of his erotic life, standing on Westminster Bridge with his pocket full of lead balls, contemplating suicide because a courtesan whom he found irresistible had robbed him of his dignity and huge sums of money without ever allowing him into her bed. Sex was certainly the driving force in Casanova's life, and his success with women at every level of society was such that a single rejection was unbearable. Rescued by a passing Londoner, however, he was taken off to a sort of strip club and decided to live another day.

Casanova's private life and escapades are so engrossingly entertaining that other aspects of his truly astonishing career tend to be neglected. He was interested in mathematics, philosophy and medicine (his advancement in Venetian society was due to his saving Senator Bragadin from an almost fatal heart attack). His fascination with the theatre led to adventures as an impresario. He ran a successful silk factory and a very profitable French lottery. He was highly paid for advice on the French fleet during the Seven Years' War. And he wrote successful plays and satirical pamphlets. Indeed, the Great Panjandrum had nothing on him.

An allegedly complete *Story of My Life* was published with considerable brouhaha in the 1960s (after the appearance of 400 expurgated editions). This, I seem to remember, was a surprise – the survival of the manuscript had been kept very quiet. The twelve bundles of foolscap pages, covered on both sides in Casanova's unmistakable hand, had originally been carried off to Dresden after his death by Carlo Angiolini, the husband of a niece who had cared for the dying Casanova. His plans to publish the *Life* were scuppered by the Napoleonic Wars, and in 1821 Carlo's impoverished family sold the manuscript to Frederic-Arnold Brockhaus, the founder of a distinguished German publishing firm.

Brockhaus published editions in German and French, heavily edited and sometimes falsified; but at least the firm kept the manuscript safe. When in 1943 the Nazis closed the company, it's said that Brockhaus's descendant himself carried it off to a Leipzig bank on a bicycle, and that it later reappeared outside his office, thrown on to the back of an American army truck. If so, this was casual treatment for a manuscript which in 2010 was presented to the French National Library by a donor who is said to have bought it from the Brockhaus family for 7.2 million euros. It is claimed that the French language edition published between 2013 and 2015 is the most accurate and complete yet.

*The Story of My Life* is not in any way a pornographic book – it is an autobiography in which Casanova records his sexual adventures with frank, open delight in the pleasure he both received and gave, in language completely free of obscenity. The result, dare I say, is a great deal more successful than coarser texts in defining what might be called the joy of sex. Abridged versions which attempt to 'clean the book up' – including the Penguin Classics edition – are like an omelette made with powdered egg.

Though in terms of today's attitudes some of Casanova's amorous exploits are far from acceptable, a modern reader will still find it a difficult book to put down. Casanova is too good a storyteller for that. When he was 15, a proud young abbé, angelically handsome with beautifully curled, scented hair falling to his shoulders, he preached a sermon in a Venetian church. The church was crowded with women; the collection purse contained the equivalent, today, of over £2,000. Now read on.

DEREK PARKER's biography, *Casanova*, was published in 2002, and his *Conversations with Casanova* in 2019.

# A Place to Call His Own

SUE GEE

He had thought deeply about this house, and knew exactly what he wanted. He wanted, in the first place, a real house, made with real materials. He didn't want mud for walls, earth for floor, tree branches for rafters and grass for roof. He wanted wooden walls, all tongue-and-groove. He wanted a galvanised roof and a wooden ceiling . . . The kitchen would be a shed in the yard; a neat shed, connected to the house by a covered way. And his house would be painted. The roof would be red, the outside walls ochre and the windows white.

*A House for Mr Biswas* was my lockdown book. As cases of Covid climbed, and the loveliest spring was filled with fear, I took myself back to the first half of the twentieth century, and to post-colonial Trinidad. Here, in a rural backwater, on an uncertain day in an unnamed year, a baby is born to a life of struggle and anxiety.

Trinidad, a Caribbean island off the coast of Venezuela, was colonized first by the Spanish, then the French and then the British. It was a place which oil eventually made rich but where much of the population had always lived in poverty; where from the late nineteenth century Indian indentured labourers worked on the sugar-cane plantations, replacing the African slaves who were finally, in 1834, granted emancipation throughout the British Empire. In truth, these new arrivals, transported in terrible

V. S. Naipaul, *A House for Mr Biswas* (1961)
Picador · Pb · 640pp · £10.99 · ISBN 9781509803507

conditions, lived lives which were not so far from slavery.

Two such labourers were V. S. Naipaul's maternal grandparents: high-caste Hindus. His father, Seepersad, whose own Indian origins are uncertain, and who began his working life as a sign-painter, married one of their daughters in 1929. In so doing, he entered a large, commanding, matriarchal family who supported him but often made his life unendurable.

*A House for Mr Biswas* is a portrait of this clever, difficult, fragile man, struggling for autonomy in impossible circumstances. Published by André Deutsch in 1961, the book began for Naipaul with the poignant recollection of the handful of household goods and furniture – a meat safe, a chair, a bookcase and hat rack – which accompanied his parents with every move they made. Gradually, these simple things opened up a great seam of memory, transformed, through the workings of imagination, into art.

> 'You see, Ma. I have no father to look after me and people can treat me how they want . . . I am going to get a job on my own. And I am going to get my own house, too. I am finished with this.' He waved his aching arm about the mud walls and the low, sooty thatch.

In a different time, and in a different diction, the words could be spoken by David Copperfield. Seepersad, a fine writer himself who became a journalist, was entranced by Dickens, and the crowded, epic sweep of this book, with a vulnerable, tragi-comic hero whom we grow to love, can only be described as Dickensian. As the African-American writer Teju Cole expresses it in his magnificent introduction to my Picador Classic edition, *A House for Mr Biswas* 'brings to startling fruition in twentieth-century Trinidad the promise of the nineteenth-century European novel'.

Naipaul's work is a mighty creation, revealing an entire world through the experience of a kind of Everyman – someone who yearns for the one thing everyone needs: a home. It takes five moves and several jobs, over decades, before he can close his own, ill-fitting front door.

The Monday morning after his outburst to his mother, Mr Biswas sets forth. He is perhaps 16, and only as a baby has he known any kind of tenderness. He has been educated in colonial style with the recital of tables, an introduction to oases, igloos and the Great War, via 'the Lord's Prayer in Hindi from the *King George V Hindi Reader*'. His only gift has been in lettering, for which he has great feeling.

'How did one look for a job? He supposed that one looked. He walked up and down the Main Road, looking.' The road is hot, crowded, noisy. He passes tailors, undertakers, gloomy dry-goods shops, vegetable stalls whose holders stare at him. He can imagine himself in none of these places, and returns to tell his mother, 'I am not going to take any job at all. I am going to kill myself.'

It is an old schoolfriend, working as a sign-painter, who rescues him, taking him on as his assistant. Through this job Biswas meets Shama Tulsi, a silent, pretty young girl working in the cavernous family store, with whom he stumbles into marriage. Here is the first of his moves: from his mother's dark little hut to Hanuman House, the Tulsi family home.

'[The Tulsis] had some reputation among Hindus as a pious, landowning family.' They certainly have money, though no one is quite certain where first it came from. Their house, 'an alien white fortress', is crowned with a statue of the Hindu monkey-god Hanuman, affording an enraged or irritable Mr Biswas many opportunities to call it a monkey-house.

The family is enormous: countless married daughters and their offspring, and two ambitious sons who are treated like gods. An undifferentiated mass of malnourished children peep out from doorways, scamper laughing into the yard, sleep in rows on the upper floor, weep when they are beaten. They are beaten (sometimes flogged) very often, something which is as much a part of daily life as the women's endless cooking, the demanding return of their husbands from the fields. Every man, noisily eating rice and vegetables from brass plates, is assiduously attended to by his wife.

Mr Biswas dislikes eating off brass plates and dislikes the food. He is often to be found in retreat, lying on his bed upstairs in vest and underpants (made from flour sacks, the lettering still visible, to general hilarity) reading the *Meditations* of Marcus Aurelius. It is not long before he becomes the buffoon intruder, and after a fight is evicted, though Mrs Tulsi sets him up in a scrap of a shop, 'a short, narrow room with a rusty galvanised iron roof'.

By now Shama is pregnant. Her frequent return to Hanuman House after their first daughter is born, and subsequent return to Mr Biswas, sets the pattern for their marriage: immensely difficult but, in spite of everything, enduring. Shama emerges as capable and strong, sometimes even kind, and she knows him through and through. Their exchanges are often tough, and very funny.

'And how the old queen?' That was Mrs Tulsi. 'The old hen? The old cow?'

'Well, nobody did ask you to get married into this family, you know.'

'Family? Family? This blasted fowlrun you calling family?'

Six years in the oppressive little shop, where Mr Biswas commissions a house which is never finished, are followed by a move of the entire family to Green Vale, close to the Tulsi plantation. Now working as a sub-overseer, Biswas is housed in a barrack room whose every wall is lined with newspapers and cut-off headlines. AMAZING SCENES WERE WITNESSED YESTERDAY WHEN. These words sink into him for ever. In another family move, this time to the hills, he builds another house, which is destroyed by fire. Despair engulfs him.

By now, three more children have arrived, the second a boy, Anand. Like Naipaul, he will one day win a scholarship to Oxford. His developing patience with his father's often outrageously difficult temperament, when he himself is suffering, is one of the most moving threads of the novel.

Eventually, Biswas storms from the Tulsi household. Alone and furious, he leaves at last the huts, the dusty roads, the acres of sugar-cane and the buffalo-carts of village life, discovering 'the shops and cafés and buses, cars, trams and bicycles, horns and bells and shouts' of the streets of Port of Spain, the island's little capital. Here, from the open windows of the newspaper offices, he hears machinery rattling and inhales the warm smell of oil, ink and paper.

And here the sign-writing job he took almost by accident proves to be the most useful training he could have had. As a sign-writer he is taken on by the *Sentinel* – Naipaul's version of the *Trinidad Guardian*, where his father worked – and when he submits a story along the line of AMAZING SCENES he is given a chance as a journalist. He has entered at last the dreamed-of world of writing. Books, since his youth, have sustained and comforted him. He sends for his family. I will leave the reader to discover, years later, the gimcrack place he can finally call his own, and the understated tenderness of the novel's ending.

Naipaul described his father's reading to him when he was a little boy as offering 'the richest imaginative experience of my childhood'. As an adult, he often distanced himself from Trinidad. Yet he once wrote that 'Half of a writer's work . . . is the discovery of his subject.' Following the instruction of his yearning, frustrated father, to 'write about what you know', he made his discovery.

And knowing everything about the place where he grew up – its hot, crowded city streets; 'the flat acres of sugar-cane and the muddy ricelands'; the shouting and stoicism of Hindu family life – interweaving it all with the universals of human suffering and endurance, he created in *A House for Mr Biswas* what Teju Cole has called one of the imperishable novels of the twentieth century.

SUE GEE was conceived in India and born in Dorking. Her novel *Coming Home* (2013) tries to come to terms with this.

# *Peak Experience*

MARGARET VON KLEMPERER

I have a childhood memory of being ill in bed, bored and grumpy until my mother came up with an idea of genius. This must have been in late 1953 or 1954 because we had a children's version of *The Ascent of Everest* and, like most people at the time, were captivated by the conquest of the world's highest mountain. My mother showed me how to position my knees under the eiderdown, roped two miniature naked pink plastic figures together with blue wool and we re-enacted the ascent. Through the Khumbu icefall, up the South Col and the Hillary Step and on to the summit. The magic of those names.

It was a game that kept me entranced for hours and inspired my lifelong interest in the literature of mountaineering, despite a deep-rooted dislike both of heights and of being cold and uncomfortable. Sherpa Tenzing Norgay was my hero, and in all my ascents, he, naked and bright pink, reached the summit first.

And so it began. Over the years I read about Mallory and Irvine, followed Eric Shipton's exploits in the Himalayas, felt the hair on the back of my neck prickle as I struggled off a Peruvian mountain with Joe Simpson, broken leg and all. But only later did I find a copy of *No Picnic on Mount Kenya* (1952) by Felice Benuzzi, though I already knew of the book. My parents had both been stationed in Kenya during the Second World War – it was where they met and married – and I remember hearing them reminisce about the stir Benuzzi's adventure had caused during the war.

---

Felice Benuzzi, *No Picnic on Mount Kenya* (English edition 1952)
MacLehose Press · Pb · 336pp · £12.99 · ISBN 9780857053770

Felice Benuzzi was an officer in the Italian Colonial Service in Abyssinia. He was captured by the British in 1941 and ended up in a POW camp in Nanyuki at the foot of Mount Kenya. Benuzzi was an experienced mountaineer, with climbs in the Dolomites and the Alps to his credit, and when he caught a glimpse of the summit of Mount Kenya emerging from its encircling wreath of cloud, the vegetative state of captivity he describes took on a new dimension. Escape was a possibility – not to attempt the 1,000-mile hike to neutral Portuguese East Africa, but to climb the beautiful, snow-capped peak that sits on the Equator with one face looking towards each hemisphere, and then return to the camp. It would be an adventure, a way to snap the shackles of imprisonment.

> In order to break the monotony of life one had only to start taking risks again, to try to get out of this Noah's Ark, which was preserving us from the risks of war but isolating us from the world, to get out into the deluge of life. If there is no means of escaping to a neutral country . . . then, I thought, at least I shall stage a break in this awful travesty of life. I shall try to get out, climb Mount Kenya and return here.

Having seen the peak, Benuzzi began his preparations. Finding companions wasn't easy – some competent climbers thought he was completely insane. But eventually he assembled a team of three – himself, Giuàn Balletto who was a doctor and fellow climber, and Enzo Bassotti, not a mountaineer but needed as a third man to stay at base camp while the other two made the final assault on the peak. Equipment, including home-made crampons and ice-axes, warm clothes and food, was 'liberated', bartered for, made or otherwise acquired and plans were set in motion.

Benuzzi and his companions rejected the idea of bribing the guards to make their escape: they considered that to be 'low'. This is one instance of the faint flavour of *Boy's Own* adventuring that surrounds the whole escapade. However, it is underpinned throughout by a more spiritual, thoughtful atmosphere. It is this juxtaposition that gives Benuzzi's book so much of its appeal. Adventure sure enough, but with a more profound soul.

Once out of the camp, via the vegetable garden where they were allowed to work, the escapees had to get through an inhabited area, walking at night. After that the danger was nature itself. Mount Kenya is home to big and dangerous animals – elephant, rhino, leopard and the like. Benuzzi and his companions had seen a small-scale map taken from a book, and they had a profile of the mountain from the side they couldn't see, the trademark label from a tin of Kenylon Meat and Vegetable Rations, a brand made by Oxo. It was not a well-equipped expedition by any means, but what mattered to the trio was the sense of being in control of their own destiny.

> As knights of old crossed perilous seas, fought fiery dragons and even each other, for the love of their princesses, so nowadays mountaineers armed with ice-axes and ropes, crampons and pitons, make dangerous and wearisome journeys and endure every hardship for the sake of their mountains. And in winning their beloved, many of them lose their lives.

No lives were lost on this expedition, but they came pretty close.

Following the glacial streams up the mountain, they passed through forests of bamboo and giant heather. Benuzzi manages to create a sense of wonder rather than a litany of hard slog, though make no mistake, hard slog it was:

> Every step led to new discoveries, and we were continually in a state of amazed admiration and gratitude. It was as though we were living at the beginning of time, before men had begun to give names to things.

Bassotti, unwell at the start, suffered from the altitude – Mount Kenya rises to over 17,000 feet – and everything took longer than anticipated, with dire implications for their food supplies. But they finally managed to establish a base camp for their attempt on the summit.

Faced with an unknown route and icy blizzards, Benuzzi and Balletto failed in their attempt to summit the Batian peak, the highest point on the mountain. But despite the fact that their food was almost exhausted, they decided to have a go at the lower Lenana point. It was here that they would place their home-made Italian flag,

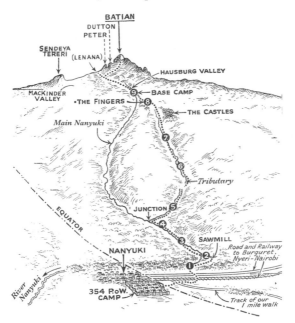

proof of what they had achieved, later to be retrieved and acknowledged, somewhat grudgingly, by the British.

> If anyone wonders what it meant to us to see the flag of our country flying free in the sky after not having seen it so for two long years, and having seen for some time previous to this only white flags, masses of them, I can only say that it was a grand sight indeed.

When climbing Lenana, the two had spotted a hut that pointed to what they correctly guessed was the established route to the summit. They were tempted to explore the hut, for it might contain some desperately needed food, and have one last shot at Batian. But they would have had no way of leaving money for the food – if there was any – and they felt that to use a British hut and steal its contents would be 'unsporting'. The standards of a bygone era.

The story of the descent is as much of an epic as the ascent. The three struggled on, getting nearer to food, but also to captivity after seventeen days of liberty. Once back, they were sentenced to twenty-eight days in the cells, though the commandant let them out after seven, in recognition of their sporting effort. But in what seems to me a very mean move the British then moved them to another POW camp, one for hard cases, where they would have no view of their mountain, and, presumably, no temptation to escape. They were to endure three more long years of captivity.

Felice Benuzzi wrote *No Picnic on Mount Kenya* twice, once in Italian and once in English, not using a translator in the usual way. When the war was over he was reunited with his family and went on to have a distinguished career as a diplomat. He died in 1988. The home-made kit from the expedition was eventually rescued from where they had left it on Mount Kenya and is now in the mountain-eering museum in Chamonix. The flag they raised on Point Lenana was returned to Benuzzi, who donated it to the museum in Turin, and a spot on the mountain was named Benuzzi Col in honour of their adventure. But the best memorial to Benuzzi and his companions is the power of their story of mountaineering adventure and what it says about human resilience.

MARGARET VON KLEMPERER grew up in the UK but has lived and worked as an arts journalist in South Africa for many years. Now retired, she loves walking among mountains, but not climbing them.

# Wheels of Fortune

JONATHAN SMITH

When publicly embarrassed by how poorly read I am, and especially so when being pressed by my family, I often claim to be rereading a book because 'it's so many years now since I first came across it'. In fact the plain truth is I haven't got a clue about the book in question because I have never opened it.

There are some books, however, that I have read and reread and I am not finished with any of them yet. A few, all of them sublimely short, would be J. L. Carr's *A Month in the Country*, Dylan Thomas's *Portrait of the Artist as a Young Dog*, Paul Scott's *Staying On* and George Eliot's *Silas Marner*. (If you want some evidence of my staying power over a longer distance, I would point to Anthony Powell's *Dance to the Music of Time*: all twelve volumes, twice.)

The first thing that caught my eye on recently opening (or reopening) *Silas Marner* was the epigraph, from Wordsworth.

> A child, more than all other gifts
> That earth can offer to declining man,
> Brings hope with it, and forward-looking thoughts.

The words not only caught my eye but held it. Old age, declining years, the gift of a child . . . how apt a quotation to place at the beginning of the tale of Silas and Eppie. But before I could even start to reread the novel, my mind was side-tracked from prose to poetry, from George Eliot to Wordsworth.

---

George Eliot, *Silas Marner: The Weaver of Raveloe* (1861)
Penguin · Pb · 272pp · £5.99 · ISBN 9780141439754

At first I could not place the lines of poetry, and this annoyed me. After all, Wordsworth is a favourite writer. I should know. But it's an age since I last taught his poem 'Michael' in the classroom. Over the years I think I rather lost confidence in teaching Wordsworth and felt – so much did he mean to me – unwilling to fight the good fight for modest plain lives, for simple childhoods, for old-fashioned stories in rural settings.

So it was high time I got my Collected Wordsworth down from the shelves.

'Michael', written in 1800, is 482 lines long and I was immediately back in the hills. Set in a precise place in the Lake District, not far from Grasmere, it is subtitled 'A pastoral poem'.

I first read it and George Eliot's rural tale at the same stage of my life. In the late 1950s I was a schoolboy in Wales, and just another muddled and preoccupied teenager (see Dylan Thomas's *Portrait of the Artist as a Young Dog*). It was a time when I was beginning to escape, sometimes (like Dylan) self-consciously striding along from Swansea to the Gower coast but usually inland on the Brecon Beacons, sometimes with friends but more often than not alone.

In the foothills of the Beacons I stepped over streams and skirted isolated farmyards and was barked at by sheepdogs. I passed places very like the shepherd Michael's cottage. On higher ground, I occasionally noticed obscure mounds of stones, places which felt special if not sacred, and uncannily close in spirit to Wordsworth's Lake District.

And, as so often when reading Wordsworth, it is the precise sense of place (take the A591 out of Grasmere) which strikes you.

> If from the public way you turn your steps
> Up the tumultuous brook of Green-head Ghyll
> You will suppose that with an upright path
> Your feet must struggle; in such bold ascent
> The pastoral mountains front you, face to face,
> But courage!

Wordsworth is walking with us, guiding our steps to the forest-side in Grasmere Vale where dwelt Michael, a shepherd.

> Nor should I have made mention of this Dell,
> But for one object which you might pass by,
> Might see and notice not. Beside the brook
> Appears a straggling heap of unhewn stones!
> And to that simple object appertains
> A story . . .

And that begins Wordsworth's story, with more than a hint of the Prodigal Son. The strong old shepherd Michael has a younger wife, 'a woman of a stirring life'. They are hard-working, thrifty people and the light of their lives is their only child, their son Luke. In him they invest their love, and the bonds between the three of them feel unbreakably strong.

Unravelling the threads and parallels and contrasts between the poem and George Eliot's novel feels right because hard-working weavers are at the heart of the matter: Isabel, Michael's wife, a comely matron twenty years younger, is (like Silas Marner) a weaver:

> Whose heart was in her house: two wheels she had
> Of antique form; this large, for spinning wool;
> This small, for flax; and, if one wheel had rest,
> It was because the other was at work . . .

Isabel and Michael are 'a proverb in the vale for their endless industry', and after supper Luke often lends his mother a hand at the fireside loom:

> There by the light of this old lamp they sate,
> Father and Son, while far into the night
> The Housewife plied her own peculiar work,
> Making the cottage through the silent hours
> Murmur as with the sound of summer flies.

A tale which promises a happy ending for 440 lines is, however, brought to a brutally shocking conclusion when the 18-year-old Luke goes off the rails. It is heavy news. After all the years of quiet and deep parental care, after ten pages of poetry, comes the car crash. The family's sad fate takes Wordsworth only six plain, unsparing lines:

> Meantime Luke began
> To slacken in his duty; and, at length,
> He in the dissolute city gave himself
> To evil courses: ignominy and shame
> Fell on him, so that he was driven at last
> To seek a hiding-place beyond the seas.

How different an ending it is for Silas.

*Silas Marner* (1861), published sixty years after 'Michael', and George Eliot's most strongly poetic novel, can be seen as her own lyrical ballad, a reading her epigraph from Wordsworth surely invites.

As well as walking the Welsh hills in the 1950s, I was beginning to read George Eliot in a serious way. I started with *The Mill on the Floss*, which hit me hard, and then, as a set book for A Level, I moved on to *Middlemarch*, which remains an unmatched experience, but as I have grown older in my body and younger (I hope) in my mind, it is the fate of the wronged Weaver of Raveloe that pulls most at me. Her third novel stays so clearly woven and interwoven into my memory. As I reread it, George Eliot invited me to sit at Silas's spinning wheel, to live his solitary days in solitary ways, to be a man with no wife and no child, to feel what it is to be a disinherited remnant, and to embrace the isolated, the unknown and the unlike.

I have never been able to shake off the story of that stranger, Silas Marner, that pallid, short-sighted, mysterious, under-sized man who (earlier in his life) has been falsely accused of theft and cast out by a narrow religious sect.

Short though it is, the novel opens out into the loving story of Silas and Eppie, the golden-haired child, as well as the story of the

Cass brothers, the fate of Molly and of Nancy Lammeter, indeed into a portrait of the whole close-knit Raveloe community from squire to pub. It is on a much smaller scale than *Middlemarch*, of course, but as short and as fine as *Middlemarch* is long. Indeed, we know from her letters that George Eliot initially considered writing *Silas Marner* as a poem. Is it, in a sense, her response to 'Michael'?

Wordsworth's old shepherd is left alone with a pile of stones, sitting with his faithful dog by the sheepfold that he and Luke would never finish building. He is an object of pity. With the Weaver of Raveloe the opposite is the case: Silas is protected by love, and chosen by his 'daughter' Eppie, who rejects the offer of a comfortable materialistic life with her natural father, Godfrey Cass.

Things turn out well for Silas, then, as he deserves. In time he is integrated into the community. His years of loneliness and self-isolation are transformed as Raveloe comes to accept him, even to embrace him. His tortured soul is repaired.

Sentimental? Is it a sentimental thing to believe that love has more meaning and more value than coins, however brightly they shine in your hands and however high the heap under your floorboards? Is it sentimental to picture a drug-addicted mother dying in the snow while her child crawls to safety and a life of warm support? Is it sentimental to see that 'natural human relations' are vital to awakening love in – and restoring dignity to – a damaged and anguished person? Do we not treasure such blessings and renewals in our own shared lives?

Even to ask such rhetorical questions may sound priggish or smack of the pulpit but Wordsworth and George Eliot, whatever the varying and changing nature of their religious convictions, were ethical teachers. Open their work on any page, and you will find moral choices moulding human destinies.

JONATHAN SMITH taught English at Tonbridge School. His latest book, *Being Betjeman*, was published by Galileo, Cambridge, in 2020.

# *What We Have Lost*

### JIM CRUMLEY

*Ring of Bright Water* caught me off guard. Gavin Maxwell's memorial to a year of his life shared with an otter and glorious secular hymn to the West Highland seaboard of Scotland hit me between the eyes, thumped me in the solar plexus, then threw a bucket of cold water over me. So I sat up and read it again.

I was about 20. I had been working as a trainee journalist since I was 16 in the epicentre of Scottish journalism which is Dundee, home to D. C. Thomson, and where I was born, grew up and lived for the first twenty-one years of my life. It was an upbringing as solidly East Coast and un-Highland as red sandstone cliffs and Arbroath smokies. But I had dipped a toe in West Highland waters on family holidays, and it's fair to say that I craved immersion.

I was idealistic, impressionable, addicted to an intoxicating broth of a fantasy Highland idyll and the dazzling journalism of such as James Cameron, John Rafferty, Michael Frayn and Michael Parkinson (and yes *that* Michael Frayn and Michael Parkinson; it was fifty-something years ago). I was ripe for exploitation by something life-defining. It would turn out to be *Ring of Bright Water* (1960), which I picked up in the first place only because I liked the title. By the time I had read the Foreword, in particular a passage I have read so often in the intervening decades that I know it by heart, I was smitten:

For I am convinced that man has suffered in his separation

Gavin Maxwell, *Ring of Bright Water* (1960)
Little Toller · Pb · 224pp · £14 · ISBN 9780956254504

from the soil and from the other living creatures of the world; the evolution of his intellect has outrun his needs as an animal, and as yet he must still, for security, look long on some portion of the earth as it was before he tampered with it.

By the time I reached the end of the book – twice – I no longer wanted to write like Cameron, Rafferty, Frayn or Parkinson. Instead, a single idea had coalesced in my scrambled brain: 'I want to look long on some portion of the earth.'

It took me another twenty years of newspaper life before circumstances permitted the required leap of faith and I sailed to St Kilda with a commission to write my first book. Now I have just written my fortieth, and my awareness of an unpayable debt to *Ring of Bright Water* only deepens.

The book has travelled the world and sold 2 million copies. Generation after generation has been inspired by the possibilities it offers, by the dreams it ignites. Ask them what they think the book is about and most people will say 'otters', and of course it is, but *Ring of Bright Water* is two books in one, or perhaps even three. Yes, the word 'otter' appears in the first line of the first chapter, but it doesn't appear again until p.74, more than a third of the way through the book. For the first third, Gavin Maxwell is setting the scene, telling stories and, especially, painting landscape pictures, for he was an accomplished artist and his book is written with a painter's eye.  By the time otters enter the narrative, you are captive in his landscape of unfurling wonder. *Ring of Bright Water* is what the poet and illustrator Margiad Evans called 'earth writing', exalted to literature, a book about one man's relationship with a truly wild and beautiful landscape and the creatures that frequent it simply because they need to be there, and these (you will agree long before the end of the book) would have to include Gavin Maxwell. Then there are the creatures he added to the mix, some young greylag geese he more or less taught to fly; some otters.

When Maxwell arrived at Sandaig on the West Highland coast opposite Skye in the late 1950s, he was a man who had suffered in his separation from the soil and the other living creatures of the world, who needed to look long at some portion of the earth as it was before he tampered with it. His first response to the place he called Camusfearna is like a rapidly executed watercolour: eyes flicker from house to islands . . . white sands to flat green pasture round the croft . . . wheeling gulls . . . pale satin sea . . . snow-topped Skye Cuillin. Then he begins to fill in the principal details. The result materializes before your eyes, beautiful and breathless and yes, painterly. Then the pace changes and it suddenly all comes to a dead stop at one of those remarkable writerly flourishes with which the whole book is peppered:

> Even at a distance Camusfearna house wore that strange look that comes to dwellings after long disuse. It is indefinable, and it is not produced by obvious signs of neglect; Camusfearna had few slates missing from the roof and the windows were all intact, but the house wore that secretive expression that is in some way akin to a young girl's face during her first pregnancy.

The intimacies of the landscape and Maxwell's responses to it are revealed bit by bit. The third chapter is pivotal, for this is when the writing shifts up a gear and at the same time (it is surely no coincidence) you are left in no doubt that the character of the place is determined by water on the move. There are two pages about the waterfall that live with you for weeks after you finish reading, and just as Maxwell called it Camusfearna's 'soul', you may consider that those two pages are the soul of *Ring of Bright Water*. But you may consider later that it has more than one soul.

It is followed almost at once by three pages about seashells, which you might think excessive, but if you like your earth writing knee-deep in tidepools, you are sorry when the chapter ends, for it is a little masterclass you have just waded through. Maxwell introduces it thus:

There is a perpetual mystery and excitement in living on the seashore, which is in part a return to childhood and in part because for all of us the sea's edge remains the edge of the unknown . . .

The adult who retains wonder brings to his gaze some partial knowledge which can but increase it, and he brings, too, the eye of association and of symbolism, so that at the edge of the ocean he stands at the brink of his own unconscious.

Otters, when they finally move centre-stage, make a very low-profile entrance. In 1956 Gavin Maxwell had been in the marshes of southern Iraq with Wilfred Thesiger (a foray that would produce a quietist masterpiece of travel writing, *A Reed Shaken by the Wind*). The trip was at least in part an attempt to divert his mind from the death of his dog, a loss so profound that he vowed never to have another. With no preamble, Maxwell wrote:

> By then it had crossed my mind, though with no great emphasis, that I should like to keep an otter instead of a dog, and that Camusfearna, ringed by water a stone's throw from its door, would be an eminently suitable spot for this experiment. I mentioned this casually to Wilfred . . . and he, as casually, had replied that I had better get one in the Tigris marshes before I came home, for there they are as common as mosquitoes, and were often tamed by Arabs.

Near the end of his stay, and in the improbable setting of the Consulate-General in Basra (he was nothing if not well-connected), Maxwell returned to his room to find two Marsh Arabs squatting on the floor with a sack that 'squirmed from time to time' and a note from Thesiger that began 'Here is your otter . . .'

'With the opening of that sack', wrote Maxwell, 'began a phase of my life that in the essential sense has not yet ended. And may, for all I know, not end before I do. It is, in effect, a thralldom to otters, an otter fixation . . .' And so Mijbil – Mij – entered his life and heart, and thus were the seeds of literature sown and fertilized.

The thirty pages that deal with Mij at Camusfearna are as brief a part of the book as the otter's life in that landscape had been – barely a year, by which time he had taken to wandering widely and was killed in a ditch by a road-mender. But such is the quality of the writing in those few pages, so unlike anything else in the literature of the land before or since, that I believe it cemented the book's reputation and won its millions of admirers. And perhaps that is the book's second 'soul'. Its essence is the relationship between a man and a wild animal, elevated to a pitch which most of us would have thought was impossible. A kind of rainbow moment sets the writer's seal on that relationship. Mij had been missing overnight for the first time and Maxwell had feared the worst. He had searched all night and all the following day, and when Mij finally walked back into the house, the reunion had been boisterous and ecstatic. Then there was this:

I am aware that this scene of reunion, and the hours that for me had preceded it, must appear to many a reader little short of nauseous. I might write of it and subsequent events with a wry dishonesty, a negation of my feeling for that creature, which might disarm criticism, might forestall the accusation of sentimentality and slushiness to which I now lay myself open. There is, however, a certain obligation of honesty upon a writer, without which his words are worthless, and beyond that my feeling for animals that I adopt would, despite any dissimulation that I might essay, reveal itself as intense, even crucial. I knew by that time that Mij meant more to me than most human beings of my acquaintance, that I should miss his physical presence more than theirs, and I was not ashamed of it. In the penultimate analysis, perhaps, I knew that Mij trusted me more utterly than did any of my own kind, and so supplied a need that we are slow to admit.

There it is, Gavin Maxwell's single most telling 'for instance' of that crucial sentiment in the Foreword, not so much about mankind's relationship with the soil (echoes of which are in almost every page), but rather about the other creatures of the earth, and especially about mankind's own needs as an animal.

*Ring of Bright Water* has a threefold legacy. First, it stands as a high-water mark in the literature of the land – whether Scotland or elsewhere. Second, it transformed the fortunes of otters throughout Britain. When it was written, otters were still widely regarded as vermin, which is unarguably one of the most obnoxious words in our language, and is shorthand for a concept that excuses the routine killing of wild creatures because they happen to be inconvenient for some perversion of land use. *Ring of Bright Water* established the otter as a creature worthy of our highest endeavours in the field of nature conservation and led directly to its legal protection. And third, permit me one final reference to the Foreword's observation that man has suffered in his separation from the soil and the other creatures of the earth . . . Is that single idea not exactly what is at the heart of the 'rewilding' movement in Britain today? The option of looking on some portion of the earth as it was before we tampered with it is more or less lost to us now. But not a moment too soon, we have woken up to the possibilities of taking land that we ruined by tampering with it, and thoughtfully tampering with it again, this time to serve nature's ends rather than our own, so that it will once again resemble its former self.

I never wanted to keep an otter, far less share my bed with one; but to write of a closer, hand-in-hand walk with nature, that seemed to me an enlightened task. More than anyone else, Gavin Maxwell taught me that.

JIM CRUMLEY is a Scottish nature writer. His newly completed quartet based on the seasons – *The Nature of Autumn*, . . . *Winter*, . . . *Spring* and . . . *Summer* – was published in 2020. He is also a columnist in *The Scots Magazine*.
The illustrations in this article are by Gavin Maxwell.

# Hearing Distant Thunder

GILLIAN TINDALL

A friend at college many decades ago was the daughter of a respected Kensington GP who was deeply involved in the history of the area. On one occasion when I was visiting she mentioned that her father was discreetly relieved at the recent death of a particularly eccentric and demanding patient, a novelist who, as a leading light also of the local history society, had had to be treated with especial tact.

'Who was she?' I asked.

'Oh, she's mildly famous, I think, but you've probably not heard of her. I wouldn't have except that she's been the bane of Daddy's life. Rachel Ferguson.'

Rachel Ferguson! My absolutely favourite author from the time (aged 12 or 13) when I graduated from E. Nesbit to nibbling at books written for grown-ups (or ostensibly for grown-ups, but we will come to that). And so she was dead, and now I would never be able to meet her and tell her how much I admired the way in which she evoked the special character and atmosphere of places – Kensington in particular, in both the nineteenth and twentieth centuries, but also riverside suburbs and seaside resorts, the backstage of theatres, and grand houses where the events of long ago have left their mark. As a

---

Rachel Ferguson, *A Harp in Lowndes Square* (1936), *A Footman for the Peacock* (1940) and *Evenfield* (1942) are available in paperback from the Dean Street Press. *Alas, Poor Lady* (1937) has been reissued as a paperback by Persephone. *The Brontës Went to Woolworths* (1931) is available in paperback from Bloomsbury. *Sea Front* (1954) and *We Were Amused* (1958) are out of print, but we can obtain second-hand copies.

bored and lonely teenager imprisoned in a badly run girls' boarding school, I had empathized deeply with the aching spinsterhood of *Alas, Poor Lady* (1937) and had longed, like the main characters of *The Brontës Went to Woolworths* (1931), to be friends with actors, singers and comedians. But most of all I had been fascinated by *A Harp in Lowndes Square* (1936), in which, more than any other novel of hers, the past is not dead but is both recoverable and surmountable.

In *A Harp* a character suggests that fragmented dead voices might be picked up – perhaps through the use of a wireless, then a relatively new invention – if one went to the right location, even if the four walls that had once contained those voices had been pulled down. Later in the novel the two central figures, brother and sister, achieve this in various historic locations, including Hampton Court and a Victorian music hall, but also, and most significantly, in the large Lowndes Square house still owned and lived in by their redoubtably unpleasant grandmother.

Here, on semi-clandestine night visits, they manage not only to hear but also eventually to see partial and ghostly re-enactments of a violent event involving the grandmother from forty years before – though the word 'ghost' is never actually mentioned. Brother and sister confront the grandmother about her treatment of one of her daughters, who died as a result of what had happened. The suggestion (never made quite explicit) is that, by doing so, they can help their own elder sister, who has seemed to suffer from some mysterious vulnerability, finally to put the inherited past behind her. Again, the word 'reincarnation' is not actually used, but there is a clear indication that this is the territory in which we are moving.

Similarly, in *A Footman for the Peacock* (1940), which also deals with bygone evil, there is a definite sense of a building, this time a classic country house, retaining the memory of past events in a way that affects current occupants. We begin to realize that a young man and a girl are, unknowingly, re-enacting events in past lives, or are at any rate in danger of doing so. But the story is set in the summer of

1939, and the rapidly evolving events of that summer are used to indicate breaking moulds and impending social changes which will probably save the couple from a repetition of the past.

Between the two world wars, J. W. Dunne's *An Experiment with Time*, in which he conceived time to be circular rather than linear, aroused enduring interest and inspired, among other things, three plays by J. B. Priestley. It also clearly inspired Ferguson. In what is perhaps her most deeply eccentric novel, *The Brontës Went to Woolworths*, the main characters live their intimate family lives in an invented saga to do with famous people whom they do not actually know, and with the illustrious dead. Then, as if some unseen power struggle were going on, they are visited, fleetingly, by the Brontë sisters.

Fantasy here coincides with an apparent and slightly frightening supernatural reality – or does it? Is this another of the narrator's extensive pretend games that do, sometimes, become real? The entire (all female) family are involved in a pretend game about being close friends with a famous star of the stage: then the younger sister finds herself working with him and falling half in love. They also have a game about being friends with a High Court judge and his wife, and here, too, the pretence metamorphoses improbably into a genial reality.

In *A Harp in Lowndes Square* the fantasy is more restrained, plausible and targeted, but certain elements, in particular Ferguson's romantic passion for actors in general, inspired apparently by a period she spent at RADA, surface again. A matinée idol she calls Cosmo Furnival, and who surely had a real-life original, is the charming, intelligent (and safely married) object of the fictional narrator's love. I too fell in love with him. But I was 13, when being smitten by a fictional character for the want of any flesh-and-blood alternative may be excused. It did just occur to me even then that something was not quite right. Didn't grown-ups supposedly want something more than this? And my credulity was further stretched when, towards the end of the book, grandmother routed, dead and gone, and the Lowndes Square house reclaimed for benign parties full of old people in 'sequinned finery', the narrator begins seeing the by then departed Cosmo Furnival too about the place and finds herself re-enacting their earlier encounters. Still, as a teenager, I found the book, with its evocation of vanished places, scents and seasons, entirely gripping.

For Rachel Ferguson (1892–1957) was not in any general way naïve. Balked of a stage career by the outbreak of the First World War, she began her writing life as a journalist. For many years, indeed right into her sixties, she contributed to *Punch*, and some of her material was good enough to be collected and published in book form. She was also in youth determinedly 'modern' in outlook (though 'the modern girl' was a newspaper phrase she liked to flourish mockingly). In her teens she had been a fierce campaigner for women's rights and longed to be a suffragette, and later she became a leading light of the Women's Social and Political Union.

Her novel *Alas, Poor Lady* is perhaps now her best-known one, since it has been seized on as a feminist document on the plight of superfluous Victorian unmarried daughters. But though a compelling read, it is shallower than her most distinctive works, since its portrait of a classic down-trodden, socially demoted governess is essentially a vignette stretched out to book length – a vignette that appears more tangentially and to greater effect in her other novels, including *A Harp in Lowndes Square* and *The Brontës Went to Woolworths*.

The author undoubtedly knew loneliness and insecurity in her own life; there are clear wish-fulfilment elements in her novels. Although she could be extremely funny about her beloved world of the theatre – see her pantomimic skit on village life, *The Late Widow Twankey* (1943) – she never seems to have achieved a close relationship within that world. She did not apparently ever have a lover, and the supportive brother-and-sister relationship in *A Harp in Lowndes Square* was not borne out in her own life: her only brother took off for South Africa as soon as he reached adulthood and stayed there. The unpleasant and domineering grandmother of Lowndes Square was, however, a reality. This lady, her mother's mother, was married to a Cumberbatch (distantly related to the present-day actor) and lived in Cadogan Place. She treated her numerous children to beatings and dry bread lunches and would jeer at them if they were ill. All this was revealed in convincing detail in Ferguson's last work, a memoir called *We Were Amused*, which was not published, probably wisely, till 1958, a year after her death.

By the 1950s, living in her beloved but changed Kensington and driving her doctor mad with her needy admiration (and her passion for cats), she was far from the would-be suffragette of her early years.

Like many good novelists, Ferguson seems to have understood complex issues better when she had a pen in her hand than in her daily life. This is evident in *A Footman for the Peacock*, where all her natural sympathies were with the right-wing owners of the country house (based on one near York, where she was actually staying when Neville Chamberlain made his we-are-now-at-war speech), but her novelist's antennae told her this world was on the brink of dissolution. Later in the war she actually addressed, as a central theme, the subject of nostalgia and the folly of attempting to recreate past relationships or situations.

This book, *Evenfield* (1942), which manages to be both a loving portrayal of her childhood home and a subtle and cumulative warning that in life we should never try to go back, is regarded by some readers as her absolute best. I admire it, and also *Sea Front* (1954), her last full-length novel, which revisits some of the same themes in a convincing but less personal way. But for me, hopelessly hooked in youth, nothing, not even those Brontës buying Christmas presents in Woolworths, quite beats the audacious originality of *A Harp in Lowndes Square*.

GILLIAN TINDALL started life as a novelist and has had many stories read on the BBC; however, her main work has been in biography and in the history of places. Her most recent book is *The Pulse Glass, and the Beat of Other Hearts*.

# *What's in a Name?*

ANTHONY QUINN

I was once interviewing Kingsley Amis when he mused, apropos of nothing, 'Quinn . . . a Manx name, isn't it?' I mumbled that I thought it was Irish myself, since that's where my forebears came from. 'Yes, from the Isle of Man,' he continued, 'derived from *McGuinn*.' Was it? The curious thing is that thirty years later I still haven't bothered to find out. It feels of no more consequence to me than taking my own fingerprint. Amis's friend Anthony Powell, a connoisseur of pedigree, would have been able to identify the name's origin and place it exactly in the social pecking order. Not high, I imagine.

But wait, what's this?

> The phrase 'a Quinn' had come to symbolize a whole class of society in my mind, just as Galsworthy uses the phrase 'Forsytes'. London was full of Quinns, eating saddle of mutton at handsome mahogany tables; going up the steps of good clubs and stepping out of quiet, expensive cars.

It comes from a novel published in 1931, *My Husband Simon*, a tyro work by Mollie Panter-Downes, who would become famous for her brilliant novella *One Fine Day* and her *London War Notes*, a collection of dispatches for the *New Yorker* from the London Blitz. I'm not sure about her analogy between Quinns and the patrician-sounding Forsytes (Soames Quinn?) but still, the name mattered enough to Mollie to choose it.

What's in a name? Something suggestive, if you're a novelist. The previous year Agatha Christie had published a book of short stories revolving around *The Mysterious Mr Quin*, the single 'n' always seeming to my eye a misspelling. Over half a century later Paul Auster picked another mysterious Mr Quinn as the protagonist for the first novel of his postmodern *New York Trilogy*. This Quinn is a writer of mystery stories. One afternoon he has an assignation with a stranger in a park:

> 'Yes, very interesting. I like your name enormously, Mr Quinn. It flies off in so many directions at once.'
>
> 'Yes, I've often noticed that myself.'
>
> 'Most people don't pay attention to such things. They think of words as stones, as great unmovable objects with no life, as monads that never change.'
>
> 'Stones can change. They can be worn away by wind and water . . .'

There's quite a lot more in this riddle-me-ree vein, but you get the point. The name crops up a fair bit in fiction, often attached to a soldier or a writer. Richard Ford in his 1981 novel *The Ultimate Good Luck* calls his Vietnam War veteran Harry Quinn. And in his quite bad thriller *The Negotiator* Frederick Forsyth gives his hero (also a 'Nam veteran, tasked with solving a kidnap crisis and thus averting World War Three or something) the single name Quinn.

William Kennedy entitled one of his novels of nineteenth-century New York *Quinn's Book*, his hero Daniel Quinn being a journalist. In Amanda Craig's nifty satire on literary London, *A Vicious Circle* (1996), the heroine is a fledgling book reviewer named Mary Quinn:

> The first few times she saw the words Mary Quinn at the top of a review, she was mesmerized. It seemed she had never seen her name before. She fell in love with it, with the beautiful symmetry of the M and the curly tail of the Q.

Put like that it *does* sound rather appealing . . . An old friend of mine, Sebastian Faulks, described a Sergeant Quinn in his novel *A Fool's Alphabet* as 'a thin, melancholy man from somewhere in the north-west'. This fellow was supposed to be 'an expert in body disposal'. Cheers!

Before this starts to sound like an essay in nominative narcissism let me revert to the theme, which is the business of naming. Personally I find that characters will only come alive once I've found their names. Sometimes it occurs to you immediately; sometimes the search goes on for weeks. And given it's a name you'll be looking at constantly for a couple of years you'd better make sure you like it. I recall a time when novelists would leaf through whole telephone directories in search of names. What do they do now that telephone directories have disappeared? My own preference is to wander about Abney Park Cemetery in north London and jot down names from the gravestones (unexpectedly soothing in these lockdown days). My last notebook entry reads: Greenland – Dredge – Dennington – Tewson – Kite – Brashier – Rodway – Remnant – Chipp – Seavol – Bidgood – Gwilt. Remnant! Where else would you end up but in a graveyard? I may not have use for any of them, but it reassures me to keep the list in reserve.

There's also the option of copying from your betters. Dickens's names are too comical and outlandish to adopt for oneself. George Eliot's are somehow too lapidary. Trollope, on the other hand, is such a fantastic and profuse namer of characters that I have to stop myself nicking from him. The Palliser novels alone are a bountiful resource. Fothergill. Bonteen. Standish. Cantrip. Maule. Vavasor. Du Boung. Collingwood. Effingham. Evidently the temptation has been overpowering, because every one of those names has appeared in a book or story by me. Has there ever been a journalist in fiction better named than Quintus Slide? Or a rakish gossip-about-town better than Dolly Longstaffe?

When George Gissing wrote *New Grub Street* (1891), about a vulnerable failing novelist called Edwin Reardon, he would little have suspected that more than a century later his namesake would reappear in a radio comedy – *Ed Reardon's Week* – about a failing freelance dogsbody living in Berkhamsted with a cat named Elgar. The first time as tragedy, the second time as farce. Either way, it has become impossible to see the name Reardon without being reminded of a certain male neediness. Gissing's mordant sense of irony is also detectable in the character of a near-destitute surgeon, who appears in a single brief scene to diagnose a man's oncoming blindness from cataracts. The luckless surgeon's name: Victor Duke.

One of the best novels I read last year was Andrew Miller's atmospheric *Now We Shall Be Entirely Free*, about a British army officer on the run following the disastrous retreat at Corunna in 1809, when atrocities were visited upon the Spanish natives. I was halfway through the book before I realized that Miller had drawn his characters' names – Lacroix, Calley, Medina – from reports on the massacre of villagers by American soldiers at My Lai during the Vietnam War. The novel, which also explores seafaring, utopian living, firearms, Regency music and nascent eye surgery, is altogether gripping; with that extra layer of historical resonance it became heartbreaking, too. Names can do that.

ANTHONY QUINN's latest novel, *London, Burning*, features yet another character's surname borrowed from Anthony Trollope.

# Bibliography

Felice Benuzzi, *No Picnic on Mount Kenya*                                    70

Anthony Burgess's Malayan trilogy: *Time for a Tiger*;
   *The Enemy in the Blanket*; *Beds in the East*            7

Giacomo Casanova: the memoirs of                                             60

Richard Cobb, *Still Life*                                                   14

Laurie Colwin, *Home Cooking*; *More Home Cooking*                           19

George Eliot, *Silas Marner*                                                 75

Rachel Ferguson: the novels of                                               86

Robert Graves, *I, Claudius*; *Claudius the God*                             25

Eda Lord, *Childsplay*                                                       44

E. O. Lorimer, *Language Hunting in the Karakorum*                           55

Rose Macaulay, *The Towers of Trebizond*                                     31

Gavin Maxwell, *Ring of Bright Water*                                        80

John Moore, *The Waters under the Earth*                                     49

V. S. Naipaul, *A House for Mr Biswas*                                       65

Anthony Quinn: on naming fictional characters                                91

Arthur Ransome, *Coot Club*; *The Big Six*                                   37

## Coming attractions

LINDA LEATHERBARROW has nightmares with Stephen King ·
DEREK PARKER meets a gentleman in Moscow · CLARISSA
BURDEN sleuths with Inspector Grant · JOHN SMART dreams
of Cheddar cheese · MARGARET DRABBLE spends time with
Doris Lessing · DANIEL CREAMER visits the Elephant Man ·
SUE GEE praises bookmarks · BRANDON ROBSHAW enjoys
*A Box of Delights*

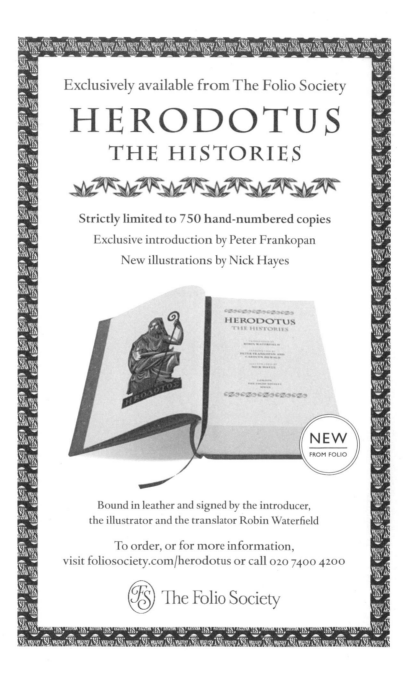